BRILLIANT COMMUNICATION

5 STEPS TO COMMUNICATING
YOUR MESSAGE CLEARLY
AND EFFECTIVELY

Patrick Forsyth

Marshall Cavendish
Business

This book was previously published as *There's No Need to Shout*
Copyright © 2011 Patrick Forsyth
Cover design: Jim Banting

Published in 2011 by Marshall Cavendish Business
An imprint of Marshall Cavendish International

PO Box 65829, London EC1P 1NY, United Kingdom
info@marshallcavendish.co.uk

and

1 New Industrial Road, Singapore 536196
genrefsales@sg.marshallcavendish.com
www.marshallcavendish.com/genref

Other Marshall Cavendish offices: Marshall Cavendish Corporation. 99 White Plains
Road, Tarrytown NY 10591-9001, USA • Marshall Cavendish International (Thailand)
Co Ltd. 253 Asoke, 12th Flr, Sukhumvit 21 Road, Klongtoey Nua, Wattana, Bangkok
10110, Thailand • Marshall Cavendish (Malaysia) Sdn Bhd. Times Subang, Lot 46,
Subang Hi-Tech Industrial Park, Batu Tiga, 40000 Shah Alam, Selangor Darul Ehsan,
Malaysia

Marshall Cavendish is a trademark of Times Publishing Limited

The right of Patrick Forsyth to be identified as the author of this work has been asserted
by him in accordance with the Copyright, Designs and Patents Act 1988.

A CIP record for this book is available from the British Library

ISBN 978-981-4351-01-0

Printed in Singapore by Fabulous Printers Pte Ltd

Contents

Introduction   5

Step 1   10
Overcoming Inherent Difficulties

Step 2   28
Preparing for Success

Step 3   41
Write Right

Step 4   77
Some Different Forms of Written Communication

Step 5   101
On Your Feet

Afterword   171

About the Author   174

Introduction

> 66 One should not aim at being possible to understand, but at being impossible to misunderstand. 99
>
> *Quintilian*

Communicating. You do it, I do it (right now, if you are reading this), and everyone around you and with whom you work, liaise, or have contact does it. We are all used to it. How can anything that is so much a part of everyday life cause problems? Yet often it does. But good communication offers many opportunities. Here, we review both the problems and the opportunities, focusing on those modes of communication that most frequently cause problems – written communication and the making of formal presentations.

The focus is on overcoming problems and making communication not only effective, but also impressive. In any organization, people are judged, in part, by how they communicate. Doing it well can enhance your profile, to the advantage of your job and career.

The pitfalls

Communication can cause problems. Offices around the world are full of people clarifying, or trying to clarify, something that has just been said: "But you said ..."; "What I meant was ..."; "You should have told me ...". Such remarks may only signify a minor glitch, and things may be quickly sorted out, with no great harm done. Even so, being known as someone who initiates such misunderstandings, and their attendant annoyance and time-wasting, is surely to be avoided. Even "minor" ineffectiveness tends to get noticed. For example, there is a hotel that has a notice inside every bedroom saying, "In the interests of security, please ensure that your bedroom door is securely closed before entering or leaving the room." Really. It would be a good trick if you could do it! But someone wrote this, got it printed and fastened to every door, and still no one noticed what nonsense it was. Never make the mistake of thinking you are too clever to do this sort of thing, saying to yourself, "I would be sure to check it." Yes, just like whoever signed off the computer manual that I have by my desk; on the first inside page is a large box in which appear the words: "This manual has been carefully for any error."

Furthermore, sometimes greater harm is done, and a lack of clear communication results in a deadline being missed, money or time lost, a customer upset, or an out-and-out row. Reprimands can follow, and reputations and careers can be threatened or, at worst, destroyed.

The potential problems of day-to-day interaction are bad enough, but when the form of communication is more demanding, the likelihood of disaster is multiplied. An ill-considered and ill-phrased report, or even memo or email, may return to haunt you weeks, months, perhaps years later. A presentation in which you dry up, omit a whole section, or display every other slide upside down, while proving inaudible at the back of the room, is going to take some living down. Even the best ideas and suggestions can be diluted so much by the way they are put over that they fail to be taken on board.

The opportunities

The ideas behind this book were prompted, in part, by a line in a training movie (*I Wasn't Prepared for That*, Video Arts) in which one character describes a presentation as "the business equivalent of an open goal." It is an apt description, and I believe it is true of communications as a whole.

Effective communication is a career skill, one affecting not only your ability to do your job, but also how likely you are to thrive and progress. Writing and presenting, the two modes of communication studied in this book, are both examples of this. On inviting people to introduce themselves and explain why they were attending a business writing course I was conducting, one person told me simply, "I'm here because I'm missing out." Asked to explain, he said that he knew that his boss regarded his reports as so appalling that he would simply not involve him in any project that involved writing one. His writing technique was adversely affecting his career in a very direct way. Similarly, anyone who has seen the bored, distracted faces in front of them as they delivered a lackluster presentation will recognize the same kind of effect linked to that mode of communication.

However, when these things are done well, the positive impact is equally direct. The good report or presentation is more likely to have its content or recommendations approved, and those who do these things well are regarded as having a greater professionalism and level of competency than others. It may not be fair, but it happens. So anyone wanting to progress in the organizational world has little option: these are things you must learn to do, and do well.

What is doing a report or presentation well? This means doing it:

- Without causing hassle to others, especially your boss
- So as to hit deadlines – every time
- With due accuracy (one spelling mistake in a report is one too many, and a key number quoted inaccurately is worse, especially if it relates to money)
- With real professionalism and, for something like a presentation, some elegance and style
- So as to be effective (people need to understand your message, perhaps to agree with it, and often to take action as a result of it)

All this means that communication must be done with confidence. Confidence stems, in part, from knowledge – knowing how to go about something in an effective way – and this book is designed to help with that. Of course, confidence and excellence increase with practice, too. It would be wrong to pretend otherwise.

But knowledge can kick-start practice and accelerate experience, so reading this book may also help.

When you finish the book, you should be in a position to communicate more effectively and impressively. In addition, when you have something substantial to do – a report to write or a presentation to prepare – you should be able to do it more quickly, something that is valuable in its own right in hectic organizational environments.

We start by reviewing key factors that explain why communication can be difficult, and consider how to minimize their impact; then we look at preparing to communicate successfully, and deal with written communication and the making of presentations.

01

Overcoming Inherent Difficulties

> **❝** If I seem unduly clear to you, you must have misunderstood what I said. **❞**
>
> *Alan Greenspan*

How would you explain, without demonstrating, how to tie a tie? How many times in the last week have you heard someone in your office protest, "But I thought you said ..."? What is the difference between describing something as "*quite* nice" and "*rather* nice"? And would you find anything that warranted either description the least bit interesting?

Make no mistake: communication can be difficult. That is the first rule.

Have you ever come out of a meeting, or put the telephone down on someone, and said to yourself, "What's the matter with that idiot? They don't seem to understand anything!" And, if so, did it cross your mind that maybe the difficulty was that you were not explaining matters as well as you could?

Make no mistake: the responsibility for making communication work lies primarily with the communicator. That is the second rule.

Put another way, the first rule about communication

is never to assume it is simple. Most of the time we spend in our offices is taken up with communicating in one way or another. It is easy to take communication for granted. Occasionally, we are not as precise as we might be, but we muddle through, and no great harm is done. Except that sometimes it is. Some communication breakdowns become out-and-out derailments.

Otherwise expressed, the second rule about communication is that the responsibility for getting through to other people – for making things clear and ensuring understanding – is *yours*. In the workplace, where there is often so much hanging on it, you need to get communication right, and the penalties for not doing so include, at best, minor disgruntlement and, at worst, major disruption to productivity or quality of work. So the second rule, that everyone needs to take responsibility for their communication, must make particular sense for all those working in organizations.

To set the scene for everything that follows, we will now consider certain key influences on whether communication works effectively or not.

THE DIFFICULTIES

If there are difficulties associated with communication, this is not because other people are especially perverse. Communication is, in fact, *inherently difficult*.

In communicating with people, what you do is essentially a part of the process of achieving your job objectives. You need to make sure that people:

1. Hear what you say, and so listen.
2. Understand clearly what you are saying.
3. Give feedback.
4. Take action in response.

Such action could be a whole range of things, for example agreeing to spend more time on something, attending a meeting, or following specific instructions.

Let us consider the four objectives in turn.

Objective 1: To ensure people listen
DIFFICULTIES AND REMEDIES

- **People cannot, or will not, concentrate for long periods of time.** This fact must be accommodated by the way we communicate. Long monologues are out; written communication should have plenty of breaks, headings, and fresh starts (like this book); and two-way conversation must be used to prevent people feeling like they are pinned down, listening to an interminable monologue

- **People pay less attention to those elements of a communication that appear unimportant.**
  So creating the right emphasis, to ensure that key points are not missed, is a key responsibility of the communicator. In other words, you have to work at making sure you are heard – to *earn* a hearing

Objective 2: To ensure people understand clearly

DIFFICULTIES AND REMEDIES

- **You may make assumptions based on your past experience.** If you wrongly assume certain experience, then your message will not make sense. Imagine trying to teach someone to drive if they had never sat in a car: "Step on the gas." "What do you mean?"

- **Jargon is often not understood.** Think very carefully about the amount of jargon you use and with whom. Jargon is professional slang, and creates a useful shorthand between people in the know, for example, in an organization or industry, but it can dilute a message if used inappropriately. For instance, used in a way that assumes a greater competency in the message's recipient than actually exists, jargon will hinder understanding. Remember, people do not like to sound stupid, and may well be reluctant to say, "I don't understand," whatever the reason for the lack of understanding

- **Messages that are heard but not seen are more easily misunderstood.** Thus, any visual aid is useful; so is a message that paints a picture in words

- **Conclusions are often drawn before a speaker finishes.** The listener is, in fact, saying to themselves, "I'm sure I can see where this is going," and their mind reduces its listening concentration, focusing instead on planning their own next comment. Be aware of this, and seek feedback on key points to make sure that the message really has got through

Objective 3: To ensure people give feedback
DIFFICULTIES AND REMEDIES

- **People sometimes deliberately hide their reactions.** You may need to read between the lines
- **Appearances can be deceptive.** For example, phrases such as "Trust me" are just as often a warning sign as a comment to be welcomed. You may have to exercise some care, if you are to appreciate the true picture

Objective 4: To ensure people take action
DIFFICULTIES AND REMEDIES

- **It is difficult to change people's habits.** Recognizing this is the first step to achieving it; a stronger case may need making than would be the case if this were not true. It also means that care must be taken to link past and future, for example, not saying, "That was wrong, and this is better," but rather, "That was fine then, but this will be better in future" (and explaining how changed circumstances make this so). Any phraseology that casts doubt on someone's earlier decisions should be avoided wherever possible
- **There may be fear of taking action.** ("Will it work? What will my colleagues think? What are the consequences of it not working out?") Risk avoidance is a natural feeling. Recognizing this, and offering appropriate reassurance, is vital
- **Many people are simply reluctant to make prompt decisions.** They may need real help from you. It is a mistake to assume that laying out an irresistible case,

and just waiting for the commitment, is all there is
to it

Key remedies: Watch and plan

The net effect of all this is rather like trying to get a clear
view through a fog. Communication goes to and fro, but
between the parties involved there is effectively a filter.
Not all of the message may get through; some parts may
be blocked, warped, or let through with bits missing.
In part, the remedy to all this is simply *watchfulness*.
If you appreciate the difficulties, you can adjust your
communication style to compensate, and achieve better
understanding as a result.

One thing is clear: *communication is likely to be better
for some planning*. This may only require a few seconds'
thought – the old premise of engaging the brain before the
mouth (or writing arm) – or it may entail making some
notes before you draft a memo or report, or even just
sitting down with a colleague to thrash out the best way to
approach something.

AIDS TO GOOD COMMUNICATION

Good communication is, in part, a matter of attention to
detail. Just using one word instead of another can make
a difference, sometimes a *significant* difference. Here are
some other major factors that influence communication.

Factor 1: What about me?

A message is more likely to be listened to and accepted if

you spell out how it affects people. They want to know, "What's in it for me?" and "How will it hurt me?" People are interested in both the potential positive and negative effects. Tell someone that you are about to introduce a new computerized reporting system, and they may well think the worst. Certainly, their reaction is unlikely to be simply, "Good for you!" It is more likely to be, "Sounds like that will be complicated" or, "Bet that will have teething troubles."

> **Build in the answers and you avert people's suspicions, making them more likely to want to take the message on board.**

Tell them they are going to find it faster and easier to submit returns using the new system. Add that it is already getting a good reaction in another department. Explain the message and what the effects on people will be, rather than leaving them wary or asking questions.

Factor 2: That's logical

The sequence and structure of communication is very important. If people know what something is, understand why it was chosen, and believe it will work *for them*, then they will pay more attention. Conversely, if it is unclear or illogical, then they worry about it, and this takes their mind off listening.

Information is remembered and used in an order –

you only have to try saying your own telephone number as quickly backward as you do forward to demonstrate this – so your selection of an appropriate order for communication will make sense to people, and they will warm to your message. Using a sensible sequence helps promote understanding, and makes it easier for people to retain and use information.

Telling people about the sequence and structure of communication is called "signposting." Say, "Let me give you some details about what the reorganization is, when the changes will come into effect, and how we will gain from it," and, provided that makes sense to your staff, they will *want* to hear what comes next. So tell them about the reorganization, and then move on. It is almost impossible to overuse signposting. It can lead into a message, giving an overview, and then separately lead into subsections of that message.

> **!** **●** Whatever you have to say, think about what you say first, second, third, and so on. Make the order you choose an appropriate sequence for your audience.

Factor 3: I can relate to that

Imagine a description: "It was a wonderful sunset." What does it make you think of? Well, a sunset, you may say. But how do you conjure up a picture of a sunset? You recall sunsets you have seen in the past (real, in movies, in art galleries), and what you imagine draws on that recollection, creating what is probably a composite based on many memories. Because it is reasonable to assume that you have seen a sunset, and enjoyed the experience, I can be fairly certain that a brief description will put what I want in your mind.

On the other hand, if I were to ask you to call to mind, say, the house in which I live, without first describing it to you, this is impossible; at least, unless you have been there, or discussed the matter with me, previously. All you can do is guess.So try to judge carefully people's prior experience; or, indeed, ask about it, if they have not worked for you for very long, and you are unsure of their past experience. Try, too, to link what you are saying to the experience of the other person, using phrases such as, "This is like ..."; "This is similar, but ...";

"You will remember ..."; "Do you know ... ?" These are all designed to help the listener grasp what you are saying more easily and accurately.

> **❗** Whatever you have to say, think about what you say first, second, third, and ● so on. Make the order you choose an appropriate sequence for your audience.

Factor 4: Say it again

Repetition is of fundamental help in grasping a point. However, it does not imply just saying the same thing, in the same words, repeatedly. Repetition takes a number of forms:

- Things repeated in different ways, or at different stages of the same conversation

- Points made in more than one manner, for example, being spoken and written down
- Summaries or checklists used to recap key points
- Reminders issued over a period of time (maybe varying the method of communication: telephone, email, or meeting)

Do not overdo repetition, but use it as a genuinely valuable aid to getting a message across. Observe how people really are more likely to retain what they take in more than once. Enough repetition.

POSITIONING YOUR COMMUNICATION

So far in this step, the principles outlined have been general; they can be useful in any communication. But differences are demanded by different circumstances. For a manager, for instance, staff are a special category. If you want people to work willingly, happily, and efficiently for you, then one useful approach to any staff communication is to remember not to allow your communication style to become too introspective. If you want to influence people, you need to relate to them in a way that makes them feel important. Although you speak for the organization, staff do not appreciate an unrelieved catalogue of statements that focus on your side of things:

The organization is ...

We have to make sure ...

I will be able to ...

Our service in the technical field is ...

My colleagues in research ...

Our organization has ...

Any such phrases can be turned around to focus on the staff, thus: "You will find this change gives you ..."; "You will receive ..."; "You can expect that ...".

A mixture of manager- and staff-centered statements is, of course, necessary, but a predominantly introspective approach can seem somewhat relentless. It is more difficult, when phrasing things that way around, for you to give a real sense of tailoring what you say to the individual; introspective statements sound very general.

! **Using the words "you" or "yours" (or similar) at the start of a message usually works well, and once this start is made, it is difficult for you to make what you say sound introspective.**

Projecting the right impression

Although it is important that you don't sound introspective, this is not to say that you should be unconcerned about the image you put across. You should be concerned about conveying the right image, and there is a good deal more to it than simply sounding or appearing pleasant.

By all means, compile your own list of suitable qualities, but you will probably want to include a need to appear:

- Efficient
- Approachable
- Knowledgeable (about whatever the situation demands)
- Well organized
- Reliable
- Consistent
- Interested in people
- Confident
- Expert (and able to offer sound advice)

You will no doubt want people to feel that they are liaising with someone competent, someone they can respect. Fair enough. But the thing to note is that, for most of us, there is a fair-sized list of characteristics that are worth getting across, and all of them are elements that can be *actively* added to the mix. You can intend to project an image of, say, confidence, and make it more than you feel, or of fairness, when you want it to be absolutely clear that this is what you are being. Projecting the right mix – and balance – of characteristics to create the right image is crucial. There is some complexity involved here, and thus it is another aspect of the whole process that deserves some active consideration.

In addition, you must have a clear vision of the way you want to project the organization you represent and the department you are in. This is especially important when you are dealing with people with whom you have less than day-to-day contact, those in other departments, for instance. Consider whether you should put over an appearance of:

- Innovation
- Long experience and substance
- Technical competency
- Having a human face
- Confidence (or whatever else)

Again, you must decide the list that suits you, and draw on it as appropriate, so as to create the total picture that is right for your audience. This is often no more than just a slight exaggeration of a characteristic, but can still be important.

In all these cases, different levels and types of people will need different points emphasizing in different ways. Some may warm to an experienced person with apparent concern for others; if so, then any qualities creating that impression should be stressed. Others may seek more weight; so a style with more telling involved makes sense for them, and you will need to suggest the clout you carry, in order to make what you say stick.

All the factors mentioned in this step are straightforward in themselves. Any complexity in making communication work comes from the need to concentrate on many things at once. Here, habit can quickly come to your assistance. There is a danger in this, too, however. Unless you maintain a conscious overview, it is easy to slip into bad habits, or, by being unthinking (and making no decision rather than the wrong decision), to allow the fine-tuning that makes for good communication to go by default. Remember, just a word or two can make a difference. A complete message delivered in an inadequate manner may cause chaos.

One other key factor in communication has not yet been given sufficient weight. As we communicate, we have to work at what occurs in both directions.

LISTENING

Clearly, listening is vital, but it is not enough just to say that. You need to make listening another *active* process. This involves:

- Concentrating on listening
- Listening very carefully
- Taking note of what is said (mentally and/or by writing notes)
- Appearing to be a good listener

Above all, adapt how you proceed in light of the information other people give, and be *perceived* to do so. Few things will endear you to others quite so much as being a good listener. It is a factor that needs only a little thought, and can quickly become a habit. It is worth a few more words.

Asking questions is one thing (see "A question of questions" opposite); listening is something else. Staff want managers to be good listeners, and managers need to be good listeners. The dangers of proceeding on assumptions, inaccurate information, or a lack of it, should be clear to us all. It is partly a matter of courtesy, and partly a matter of credibility – no one will ever feel you are taking something seriously if you appear unwilling to listen.

The need here is to *work at listening*. The following list sets out the essentials.

- **Want to listen**. This is easy once you realize how useful it is to the communication process
- **Look like a good listener**. People will appreciate it, and if they see they have your attention, they will be more forthcoming with their feedback
- **Understand.** It is not just the words, but the meaning that lies behind them, that you must note
- **React.** Let people see that you have heard, understood, and are interested. Nods, small gestures, and comments will encourage their confidence and participation
- **Stop talking.** Other than small acknowledgments, you cannot talk and listen at the same time. Do not interrupt
- **Use empathy.** Put yourself in the other person's shoes, and make sure you really appreciate their point of view
- **Check.** If necessary, ask questions promptly to clarify matters as the conversation proceeds. An understanding based even partly on guesses or assumptions is dangerous. But ask questions diplomatically; do not say, "You didn't explain that properly."
- **Remain unemotional.** Too much thinking ahead ("However can I overcome that point?") can distract you
- **Concentrate.** Allow nothing to distract you

- **Look at the other person.** An inadequate focus of attention is soon interpreted as disinterest
- **Note key points.** Edit what you hear, so that you can better retain key points
- **Avoid personalities.** Do not let your view of someone divert your attention from the message
- **Do not lose yourself in subsequent arguments.** Some thinking ahead may be useful; but too much, and you may suddenly find you have missed something
- **Avoid negatives.** Clear signs of disagreement, even just a dismissive look, can make the other person clam up, and so destroy the dialogue
- **Make notes.** Do not trust your memory. If it is polite to do so, ask permission before writing people's comments down

---

! Listening successfully is a practical
necessity if you are to excel at
● communication with people.

A QUESTION OF QUESTIONS

Before moving on, we will consider questioning techniques, which link naturally to the art of listening. Many situations need to be clarified by the asking of questions. Unless you know the facts, unless you know what people think, and, most important of all, unless you know *why* things are as they are, you may find it difficult or impossible to tackle the situation in hand. How do you resolve a dispute if you do not really understand why people are at loggerheads? How do you persuade people to take action when you do not know how they view the area in which you want them to get involved? How do managers motivate if they do not know what is important to their staff? The answer in every such case might be, "With difficulty." Questions get people talking and involved, and the answers they prompt provide the foundation for successful communication.

But questioning is more than just blurting out the first thing that comes to mind – "Why do you say that?" Even a simple phrase may carry overtones, and people wonder if you are suggesting they should not have said that, or that you see no relevance for the point made. In addition, many questions can be ambiguous. It is all too easy to ask a loosely phrased question that prompts a vague or unhelpful answer. Ask, "How long will that take?" and the reply may simply be, "Not long." Ask, "Will you finish that before I have to go to the meeting at 11:00?" and, if your purpose was to be able to prepare for the meeting accordingly, then you are much more likely to be able to decide exactly what to do.

Beyond simple clarity, you need to consider and use three distinctly different kinds of question.

- **Closed questions.** These prompt rapid yes or no answers, and are useful both as a starting point (they can be made easy to answer, so as to introduce someone gently to the questioning process), and to gain rapid confirmation of something. On the other hand, too many closed questions may create a virtual monologue, in which the questioner seems to be doing most of the talking. This can be annoying or unsatisfying to the other person

- **Open questions.** These cannot be answered with a simple yes or no, and typically begin with words like, "What," "Where," "Why," "How," "Who," and "When," and with phrases such as "Tell me about ...". Such questions get people talking, involve them, and give the conversation a feel they like. By prompting a fuller answer and encouraging people to explain, they also produce far more information than closed questions

- **Probing questions.** These are a series of linked questions designed to pursue a point. Thus a second question like, "What else is important about ... ?" or a phrase such as, "Tell me more about ..." act to get people to fill out a picture, producing both the details and reasons that lie beyond more superficial answers

It is important to give sufficient time to the questioning process, and to make it clear that sufficient time is being given. Not to do so may suggest a lack of concern. This is something that it may be useful to spell out: "I want to go through this thoroughly. I can take an hour or so now, and, if that proves inadequate, we can come back to it. Let's see how we get on."

With the need for effective listening and questioning skills, we can now turn to the preparation of messages, and consider how a little systematic thought beforehand can enhance the chances of being effective.

02

Preparing for Success

> ❝I know that you understand what you
> think I said, but I am not sure you realize that
> what you heard is not what I meant.❞
>
> *Attributed to Richard Nixon*

Enough has been said about the difficulties of communicating
effectively to demonstrate that anything and everything that
helps it go well is worth considering. In this Step, we examine
elements that are absolute fundamentals to getting it right.

Much of what is said here is generic: it helps any
communication. But you also need to adopt specific
approaches to specific tasks. Writing a report, for
instance, has some unique elements to it, as does writing
a presentation. Thus, this Step is strongly linked to others,
and it may be worth referring back to it as you study the
two modes of communication dealt with in the book.

THE ESSENTIALS

We should not think that having to prepare implies some
sort of weakness. For instance, someone you may think is
a "born" public speaker, effortlessly sailing through their
presentation, is in fact probably only able to give this
impression because they are well prepared. Preparation
needs doing; the job is to make sure it is done well.

Whether you are to write a report, make a presentation, or simply write an email or a letter, the essential preparation is the same. What does change is the complexity, and the amount of time the preparation takes. What follows in this Step relates primarily to making a presentation, but much of it applies equally to written communication.

OVERALL INTENTIONS

> **!** **Ensuring that a message is clear and unambiguous can result in positive action, so that exactly what should be done gets done.**

The clarity of a message has a demonstrable effect on what occurs next. Potential problems have already been reviewed. At best, poor communication produces confusion; at worst, it fails to get done whatever should be done. Communication is directly able to:

- Speed up action
- Improve efficiency
- Increase productivity
- Stimulate creativity

Indeed, communication must often act as a spur to whatever action is required. This is literally the case with a management communication that is an instruction. But a communication may also be designed for other purposes, such as to:

- Inform
- Motivate
- Persuade
- Change opinion
- Prompt debate or discussion
- Stimulate the generation of ideas
- Build on prior contacts or thinking

Such a list could doubtless be extended, and highlights that there is a great deal hanging on any communication. These intentions are not mutually exclusive; on many occasions, you may have more than one. It is essential to be clear about what you are trying to achieve before you communicate, if your intentions are to be achieved as you wish. Anything less causes problems; one of the reasons people spend endless time editing written documents is because the multiple intentions of each document were not clearly set out in the beginning, so the first draft ignored or short-changed one or more of these intentions.

SETTING OBJECTIVES

> **!** Whatever you may need to communicate, and however it is to be **●** done, its purpose must be clear.

You must be able to answer the key question, "Why am I doing this?" and set out a purpose, one that always needs to involve you and the recipients of your message, and describes what effect it should have on them.

Objectives not only need to be clear, but also to be spelled out in sufficient detail (certainly in your own mind, and sometimes for others). They must act as a genuine guide to what you will do. Objectives should also reflect not just what you want, but what the audience wants.

A much-quoted acronym, SMART, can provide a good guide here. This stands for:

- Specific
- Measurable
- Achievable
- Realistic
- Timed

As an example, you might regard objectives linked to your reading here about presentations, so as to:

- Enable your future presentations to come over in a way that audiences will see as appropriate and informative (*specific*)
- Ensure *measurable* action takes place afterwards – here, you might link to any appropriate measure, from agreements that group members might reach to the volume of applause received!
- Be right for you – sufficient, understandable information in manageable form that really allows you to change and improve what you do later (an *achievable* result)
- Be *realistic*, that is, desirable – hence a short text; if it

took you several days to read, then the effort might prove greater than any benefit coming from doing so

- Provide a *timed* dimension – always a good factor to include in any objective: "By when are you going to finish reading? When is your next presentation? How far ahead of it should you prepare?"

So ask yourself whether you are clear in this respect before you even begin to prepare. If you know *why* the presentation must be made, and *what* you intend to achieve, then you are well on the way to success. Time spent on clarifying or setting objectives is time well spent. This process may only take a few moments, or it may need more thought and take more time. In either case, it is still worth doing, and may well save time on later stages of preparation.

With your purpose clear, and a constant eye on the audience, you can begin to assemble your message.

CREATING THE MESSAGE

There is more to this than simply banging out the points in sequence. When writing something, do not start at the top of a clean sheet of paper (or empty screen) and just see how it goes. Similarly never write, "Ladies and gentlemen," and begin to set out a presentation in what you intend to be a verbatim way. Such an approach can lead to confusion, make significant revision necessary, and take a long time to finalize.

> **!** **A systematic approach is necessary;
> indeed, a systematic approach can
> ● quickly become a habit: that of
> preparing in a way that promptly and
> certainly enables you to deliver what you
> want.**

The following section provides a full description of a
tried-and-tested approach in six stages. It shows what to
do, and explains why this works better than a more *ad hoc*
approach. It describes the fullest degree of preparation
necessary, but does not suggest that the approach should
be followed slavishly. The important thing is to find,
experiment with, refine, and then use a method that
suits *you*. In addition, practice and experience, or other
factors such as familiarity with your chosen topic, may
well allow you to adopt a "shorthand" version of this
approach that is quicker, but still does for you the total
job that is necessary.

The approach focuses on identifying *what* the message
is to be – what you need to say, or not – and investigating
how you will put the message across. Both link to structure:
what comes first, second, and third, and what constitutes
the beginning, the middle, and the end.

There is something of a chicken-and-egg situation here.
Does preparation or an overall decision about structure
logically come first? Both are important, both are interrelated;
the sequence chosen in the six-stage approach works well,
and is intended to show the reader how to put a presentation

(or, for that matter, a written document) together. So let us move on to the detail of assembling the message.

PUTTING THE PRESENTATION TOGETHER

It is not only necessary to "engage the brain before the mouth," but also vital to think through *in advance* what a presentation must, and must not, contain. The following process of preparation is recommended solely by its practicality, and can be adapted to cope with any sort of communication – of any length, complexity, and purpose.

Accepting that preparation takes time, and building this into the business of the workplace, is the first step to being a good communicator. In the long run it saves time, in part, on the old premise that while there is never time to do things properly, time always has to be made to sort out a mess. Think about this with regard to what you do – are there things that, if skipped over, result in a much greater amount of work than would have been involved in proper preparation?

! Many communications fail, or their effectiveness is diluted, because of skimping on preparation.

The very best way of linking the principles described here to real life is to go through them with some personal project in mind, such as a presentation you are due to make, and link this to the six-stage approach that follows.

Stage 1: Listing

Forget about everything such as sequence, structure, and arrangement; just concentrate on – and list in short-note or keyword form – every significant point that your message might usefully contain. Give yourself plenty of space; something larger than the standard A4 (210 X 297mm) sheet is often useful, as it lets you see everything at a glance, without turning over pages. Set down the points as they occur to you, at random, across the page. For something simple, this might result in only a dozen words, or it might be far more.

You will find that this exercise is a good thought-prompter. It enables you to fill out the picture as one thought leads to another, with the freestyle approach removing the need to pause and try to link points or worry about sequence. With this done – and, with some presentations, it may only take a short time – you have a full picture of the possibilities for the message in front of you, and you can move on to stage 2.

Stage 2: Sorting

Now, you can review what you have noted down, and begin to bring some order to it, deciding:

- What comes first, second, and so on
- What logically links together, and how
- What supports or illustrates the points

At the same time, you can – and probably will – add some additional things, and have second thoughts about some of your original ideas, which you will delete. You need to bear in mind here what kind of duration or length you are aiming at.

This stage can often be completed in a short time by simply annotating and amending the stage 1 document. Using a second color makes this quick and easy, as do link lines, arrows, and other enhancements of the original notes.

In addition, you can begin to catch any more detailed element that comes to mind as you go through (including ways of presenting such content), noting what it is at greater length on the page or alongside.

Stage 3: Arranging

Sometimes, at the end of stage 2, you have a set of notes that are sufficiently clear, and you can start work on finalizing matters. If the notes would benefit from clarification, however, they may be worth rewriting as a neat list; or this could be the stage where you type out the notes and put them on screen, if you are working that way and want to be able to print something out in due course.

Final revision is possible as you do this; certainly, you should be left with a list reflecting the content, emphasis, level of detail, and so on that you feel is appropriate. You may well find you are pruning a bit to make things more manageable at this stage, rather than searching for additional points to make.

Stage 4: Reviewing

This may be unnecessary. Sufficient thought may have been brought to bear in earlier stages. However, for something particularly complex or important, or both, it may be worth running through again what you have noted down. Sleep on it first, perhaps – certainly, avoid finalizing the list for a moment if you have got too close to it. It is easy to find you cannot see the forest for the trees.

Make any final amendments to the list (if on screen, this should be a simple matter), and use this as your final "route map" as preparation continues.

Stage 5: Preparing the message

If it is a presentation you are preparing, it is now time to write the speaker's notes (see Step 5 for more details); if the job is to write a report or other document, then this is when you actually write it. Now you can turn your firm intentions about content into something representing not only *what* is said, but also *how* it is said.

One of the key virtues of the procedure advocated here is that it stops you trying to think about *what to say* and *how to say it* at the same time. This sounds simple and obvious, and it is, but these are two very distinct mental processes, better taken in turn. The concentration on each that such separation allows pays off in increased accuracy and effectiveness. Stage 5 must be done carefully, though the earlier work will help make it easier and quicker to get the necessary detail down.

Here are a couple of tips.

- **Choose the right moment.** There seem to be times when thoughts – and words – flow more easily than at other times. Certainly, interruptions can disrupt the flow, and make the process take much longer, as you restart again and again. The right moment, with uninterrupted time in a comfortable environment, undoubtedly helps. Given the hectic nature of most offices, it is worth some organization to achieve this

- **Keep going.** Do not pause and agonize over a phrase, heading, or other detail. You can always come back to it; indeed, it may be easier to resolve later. If you keep going, you maintain the flow, allowing consistent thinking to carry you through the structure to the end, so that you can "see" the overall shape of your piece. Once you have the main detail down, then you can go back and fine-tune, adding any final thoughts to complete the picture

Stage 6: Making a final check

> ! ● With a presentation, consider having a rehearsal, whether by talking it through to yourself, a tape recorder, or a friend/ colleague, or by going through a full-scale "dress rehearsal."

A final look (perhaps after a break) is always valuable. If an event is complex, involves a high-ranking group of people who do not meet very often, and has a great deal hanging on it, there may well be only one chance to get it right. However much preparation is done for a presentation, a rehearsal double-checks effectiveness, and is an opportunity to prompt internal feedback and create ideas to maximize success.

Thereafter, depending on the nature of the presentation, it may be useful or necessary to spend more time in revising or reading over what you plan to do. You should not overdo revision at this stage; there comes a time to be content you have it right, and to stick with it. If you are preparing a written document, then it is now that any necessary editing takes place. There will, almost certainly, be some editing – few, if any, people write text that doesn't need to be fine-tuned, in order to produce a final version.

This whole preparation process is important and not to be overlooked. Preparation does get easier, however. You will find that, with practice, you begin to produce material that needs less amendment, and that both getting it down and revising it begin to take less time.

At the end of the day, as has been said, you need to find your own version of the procedures set out here. A systematic approach helps, but the intention is not to overengineer the process. What matters is that you are comfortable with your chosen approach – that it works for you. If this is the case, then, provided your approach remains consciously designed to achieve what is necessary, it will become a habit. It will need less thinking about, yet it will still act to guarantee that you turn out something that you are content meets the needs – whatever they may be.

SUMMARY

The key issues are:

- Always to advance any thinking by devising clear objectives
- To prepare messages with a clear idea of what intentions they reflect (informing, motivating, persuading, and so on)
- To think matters through systematically, and separate decisions on *what to say* from those on *how to say it*
- To give this process sufficient time and, if possible, build in some pauses, in case you cannot see the forest for the trees
- To be prepared to fine-tune the message to get it right

Here, we have touched on the overall key issues. More detail occurs as we look at the two particular modes of communication reviewed here, though you may like to refer back to this Step later in your reading.

> ! ● Preparation is a vital part of communicating. At its simplest, it is merely a moment's constructive thought. Usually, more is necessary.

03

Write Right

66 Writing is easy; all you do is sit staring at a blank sheet of paper until the drops of blood form on your forehead. 99

Gene Fowler

In a hectic business life, writing anything can be a chore. There are surely more important things to be done: people to meet, decisions to be made, action to be taken. Yet all of these things, and more, can be dependent on written communication. A letter or memo may set up a meeting; a report may present a case and prompt a decision; a proposal may ensure certain action is taken or a particular option is selected.

But reading business papers can be a chore also, and they will not achieve their purpose unless they are read, understood, and do their job well enough to prompt the reader to action.

Business writing must *earn* a reading.

THE NATURE OF WRITTEN COMMUNICATION

You are probably both a reader and a writer of business documents. Consider the nature of the written word with your reader's hat on for a moment. Do you read everything that crosses your desk? Do you read every word of the things you do read? Do you read everything from the first word through in sequence, or do you dip into things? Almost certainly, the answers make it clear that not all writing is treated equally. Some documents are more likely to be read than others. Of course, some subjects demand your attention. Who ignores a personal note from the managing director? But the fact that some things have to be read does not make their reading any easier or more pleasurable.

Good writing, which means, not least, something that is easy to read and understand, will always be likely to get more attention than sloppy writing. Yet we all know that prevailing standards in this area are by no means universally good.

Why is this? Maybe it is education; or lack of it. Often, school assists little with the kind of writing we find ourselves having to do once we are in an organization. Maybe it is lack of feedback; perhaps managers are too tolerant of what is put in front of them. If more of it was rejected, and had to be rewritten, then more attention might be brought to bear on the task.

Habits are important here, too. We all develop a style of writing and may find it difficult to shift away from it. Worse, bad habits may be reinforced by practice. For example, word processing means that the ubiquitous standard document can often be used year after year with no one prepared to say, "Scrap it," even if they notice how inadequate it is.

A fragile process

We can all recognize the really bad report – without structure or style, but with convoluted sentences and an excess of jargon – which prompts only the one thought: "What is it trying to say?" But such documents do not have to be a complete mess to fail in their purpose. They are *inherently fragile*. One wrongly chosen word may dilute understanding, or remove what would otherwise be a positive impression made. Even something as simple as a spelling mistake (computer spell-checkers are not infallible) may have a negative effect.

I will never forget, in my first year in a consulting firm, playing a small part in proposals that were submitted to a dairy products company. After meetings, deliberations, and more meetings, a written proposal was sent. A week passed. Then an envelope arrived from the company concerned. Inside was a single sheet of paper. It was a copy of the title page of the proposal, and on it was written, in red ink, the three words "No, thank you," alongside one typed word circled in red. The word "Dairy" in the company's name had been spelled "Diary." For a long while after that, everything was checked much more carefully. The moral is clear.

As a very first rule to drum into your subconscious – check, check, and check again. Mistakes that remind of us of this are on public display, like the hotel sign mentioned in the Introduction, and a notice I saw recently in an elevator, which said, "Only use the buttons provided."

Whether the cause of a document being less good than

it should be is major or minor, the damage is the same. The quality of writing matters.

A major opportunity

Whatever the reasons for poor writing may be, suffice to say that, if prevailing standards are low, then there is a major opportunity here for those who better that standard. More so for those who excel; and, as has been said, bad documents might just come back to haunt you later.

So business writing is a vital skill. There may be a great deal hanging on a document doing the job it is intended to do – a decision, a sale, a financial result, or a personal reputation. For those who can acquire sound skills in this area, very real opportunities exist. The more you have to write, and the more important the documents you create, the truer this is. Quite simply, if you write well, then you are more likely to achieve your business goals.

This point cannot be overemphasized. One sheet of paper may not change the world, but – well written – it can influence many events in a way that affects results and those doing the writing.

And you can write well. We may not all aspire to, or succeed in, writing a great novel (mine is still on page 1), but most people can learn to turn out good business writing. Writing that is well tailored to its purpose and likely to create the effect it intends. The steps here on written communication review some of the approaches that can make business writing easier – as well as quicker (a worthwhile end in itself) – and, most importantly, that make particular documents more likely to achieve their purpose.

Good business writing need not be difficult. It is a skill: one that can be developed with study and practice. Some effort may be involved, and certainly practice helps, but it could be worse. Somerset Maugham is quoted as saying, "There are three rules for writing the novel. Unfortunately, no one knows what they are." Business writing is not so dependent on creativity, though this is involved, and it *is* subject to certain rules. Rules, of course, are made to be broken. But they do act as useful guidelines, and can therefore be a help. Here, we review how to go about the writing task, including when to follow the rules and when to break them. So what makes good business writing?

A hazardous business

Despite predictions about the "paperless office," offices seem as surrounded – submerged? – by paper as ever. Indeed, as documentation is essentially only a form of communication, this is likely to remain so. However a case is presented – even if there is no paper, as with something sent by email – it still has to be written.

With no communication, any organization is stifled. Without communication, nothing much would happen. Communication – good communication – should lubricate organizational activity and facilitate action. This is true of even the simplest memo, and is certainly so of something longer and more complex like a report.

Communication is, intrinsically, inclined to be less than

straightforward. If this is true of tiny communications, how much more potential for misunderstanding does a 25-page report present? And with written communication, the danger is that any confusion lasts. There is not necessarily an immediate opportunity to check any anomalies (the writer might be 100 miles away), and a misunderstanding on page 3 may skew the whole message taken from an entire report.

Serious, and very serious, errors

Once something is in writing, any error that causes misunderstanding is made permanent, at least for a while. The dangers of ill-thought-out writing vary.

- **It may be wrong,** but may still manage to convey its meaning, like the cookbook that advises, "To stop your eyes watering when chopping onions, put them in the freezer." It may amuse – and be a good trick if you can do it – but it will probably be understood. No great harm done, perhaps, though it might just throw doubt on the credibility of the recipe. Indeed, any fault tends to highlight the possibility of other, more serious, problems

- **It may try too hard to please,** ending up giving the wrong impression. In one hotel, there are signs on the coffee-shop tables that say, "COURTESY OF CHOICE: The concept and symbol of 'Courtesy of Choice' reflect the centuries-old philosophy that acknowledges differences while allowing them to exist together in harmony. 'Courtesy of Choice' accommodates the preferences of individuals by offering both smoking and nonsmoking areas in the spirit of conviviality and mutual respect." An absurd overpoliteness just ends up making the message sound rude – this restaurant has both smoking and nonsmoking areas, and if you find yourself next to a smoker, tough. It does matter

- **It may be incomprehensible.** A press release is an important piece of writing. One, quoted in the national press recently, was sent out by a consulting group. According to the press release, the group envisioned "a world where economic activity is ubiquitous, unbounded by the traditional definitions of commerce and universal." Er, yes – or rather, no. The newspaper referred not to the content of the press release, only to the fact that it contained a statement of such complete gobbledygook as to have no meaning at all. It is sad when any writing is so bad that it achieves less than nothing

You could doubtless extend such a list of examples *ad infinitum*. The point here is clear: it is all too easy for the written word to fail. All the above were probably the subject of some thought and checking; but not enough. Put pen to paper, and you step onto dangerous ground.

! The first requirement of good business writing is clarity.

Think of how regularly you are faced with terse, ambiguous email messages, to which you have to reply seeking clarification. Much time is wasted in this way. Similarly, a good report needs thinking about if it is to be clear. Never take for granted that understanding will be automatically generated by what you write.

It is more likely that we will give due consideration and attention to clarity if we are clear about the purpose of any document we may write.

Why are we writing?

Exactly why anything is written is important. This may seem self-evident, yet many reports, for instance, are no more than something *about* their topic. Their purpose is not clear. Without clear intentions, the tendency is for a report to ramble, to go around and around, and not come to any clear conclusion.

Documents may be written for many reasons, for example, they may intend to inform, motivate, or persuade (or any of the other intentions listed in Step 2). Often, more than one intention is aimed at, and different messages or emphasis for different people add further complexity.

Readers' expectations

If a document is to be well received, then it must meet certain expectations of its readers. Before going into these, let us consider generally what conditions such expectations. Psychologists talk about what they call the "cognitive cost." This is best explained by example. Imagine you want to program the video recorder. You want to do something that is other than routine, so you get out the instructions. Big mistake. You open them, and a double-page spread shouts at you, "This is going to be difficult!" Such a document has a high cognitive cost, that is, the cost, in time and aggravation, of understanding something. It does not appear inviting; even a cursory look is off-putting.

People are wary of this effect. They look at any document almost *expecting* that it will be hard work to read it. If they discover that the document looks easier and more inviting than they thought – in other words, that it has a low cognitive cost – then they are likely to read it with more enthusiasm. What gives people the feeling, both at first glance and as they read on, that a document is not to be avoided on principle?

In no particular order, the following are some of the key factors preferred by readers. They like writing if it is:

- **Brief.** Obviously, something short is likely to seem easier to read than something long, but what really matters is that a report or other document is of an appropriate length for its topic and purpose

- **Succinct.** This is perhaps a better word to use than "brief." It implies that a document is to the point, or long enough to say what is necessary and no more. A report may be 10 pages long, or 50, and still qualify for this description. Clearly, length is inextricably linked to message

- **Relevant.** This goes with the first two key factors. It means that a document should not be too long, and that it should cover what is required, without irrelevant content or digression. (Note: comprehensiveness is *never* an objective. If a report touched on absolutely everything, then it would certainly be too long. In fact, you always have to be selective, and if you do not say everything, then everything you do say is a choice – you need to make good content choices.)

- **Clear.** Readers must be able to understand a document. This applies in a number of ways. For example, the document should be clearly written (in the sense of not being convoluted), and use appropriate language – you should not feel that, as an intended reader, you have to look up every second word in a dictionary
- **Precise.** A document should say exactly what is necessary, and not constantly digress without purpose
- In "our" language. A document should use a level and style of language that is likely to make sense to the average reader
- **Simple.** Unnecessary complexity should be avoided
- **Well structured.** A document should proceed logically through a sequence that is clear and sensible as a way of dealing with the message
- **Descriptive.** If there is a need to paint a picture, the document must do so in a way that gets that picture over

What these key factors all have in common is that they act to make reading easier. Further, they act cumulatively, that is, the more things are right in each of these respects, the clearer the writing will be. If the impression is given that attention has *actively* been given to making the reader's task easier, so much the better.

These factors need to be tailored to the audience. Whether this is internal (say, colleagues) or external (say, customers or collaborators), you need to be clear what your communications have to do, and what kind of expectations exist at the other end. For example, a technical person will be looking for a level of detail that is clearly expressed for a report to be acceptable to them. Always focus on your audience in this way as you write.

The readers' perspective

So, good business writing must reflect the needs of the reader.

Such writing cannot be undertaken in a vacuum. It is not simply an opportunity for the writer to say things as they want. Ultimately, only readers can judge a document to be good. Thus, their perspective is the starting point, and, as the writer, you need to think about who the intended readers are, how they think, how they view the topic that you are writing about, what their experience is of the issues, and how they are likely to react to what you have to say. This perspective links to preparation, which is dealt with separately in Step 2.

Powerful habits

Habit, and the ongoing pressure of business, can combine to

push people into writing on "automatic pilot." Sometimes, if you critique something that you wrote, or that went out from your department, you can clearly see something that is wrong. A sentence does not make sense, a point fails to get across, or a description confuses rather than clarifies. Usually, the reason this has occurred is not that the writer really thought this was the best sentence, point, or description, and got it wrong. Rather, it was because there was inadequate thought of any sort; or none at all.

Habits can be difficult to break, and the end result can be a plethora of material moving around organizations couched in a kind of gobbledygook or in what some call "office-speak."

Earning a reading

The moral here is clear. Good writing does not just happen. It needs some thought and effort (and study, with which this book aims to assist). The needs requires to be actively worked at if the result is going to do the job you have in mind, and do it with some certainty.

But good habits are as powerful as bad. A shift from the latter to the former is possible, and the rewards in this case make the game very much worth the candle. Think what good writing skills can achieve.

The rewards of excellence

Consider the example of reports; they can influence action. But they also act to create an image of the writer. Within an organization of any size, people interact through communication. They send each other memos, they sit in meetings and on committees, they chat as they pass on the stairs or as they share a sandwich at lunchtime; and all of this sends out signals. It tells the world, or at least the organization, something about them. Are they knowledgeable, competent, expert, decisive, or easy to deal with? Would you take their advice, follow their lead, or support their cause?

All the different ways in which people interrelate can act together, cumulatively and progressively, to build up and maintain an image of each individual. Some ways may play a disproportionate part, and report-writing is one example. There are two reasons why this effect is important.

- Reports, unlike more transient means of communication, can last. They are passed around and considered, and remain on the record; more so if they are about important issues
- Because not everyone can write a good report, people can be impressed by a clear ability to marshal an argument and put it over in writing

Thus, reports represent an opportunity; or, in fact, two opportunities. Reports – at least, good ones – can be instrumental in prompting action; action you want, perhaps. They are also important to your profile. They say something about the kind of person you are, and how you are to work with. In a sense, there are situations where you want to make sure certain personal qualities shine through. A case may be supported by it being clear that someone who gives attention to detail, for instance, is presenting it.

Longer-term, the view taken of someone by their superiors may be influenced by their regularly reading what they regard as good reports. So next time you are burning the midnight oil to get some seemingly tedious report finalized, think of it as the business equivalent of an open goal, and remember, it could literally be affecting your chances of promotion!

Many business documents demand detailed work. Their preparation may, on occasion, seem laborious. They certainly need adequate time to be set aside for them. But as the old saying has it: if a job is worth doing, it is worth doing well. It may take no more time to prepare a good report than a lackluster one; so for any document.

If whatever you write is clear, focused, and set out so as to earn a reading, then it is more likely to achieve its purpose. In this case,

it is also more likely to act positively to enhance the profile of the writer. Both these results are surely worth while. Facing a blank sheet of paper (or, these days, screen) can be a daunting task, but go about it in the right way, and getting the words down does become possible.

WHAT TO SAY AND HOW TO SAY IT

Let us focus for a moment not on writing, but on reading, or rather readers.

Readers' likes

If you undertake to engender a totality of meaning that

corresponds with the cognition of others seeking to intake a communication from the content you display in a report, there is a greater likelihood of subsequent action being that which you desire.

You are correct. That was *not* a good start. If I want to say, "If you write well, people will understand and be more likely to react as you wish," then I should say just that. But it makes a good point with which to start this section. Language and how you use it matter. Exactly how you put things has a direct bearing on how they are received; and that, in turn, has a direct bearing on how well a report succeeds in its objectives.

It is clear that language can make a difference. That is a serious understatement; language can make a *very considerable* difference. Much that is said about language in this Step is applicable to presentations as well as written documents.

How you write must stem as much as anything from the view your intended readers have of what they want to read. Or, in some cases, are prepared to read, because – as has been said, and be honest – reading some business documents can be something of a chore; even some of those you write.

Consider four broad elements first. Readers want documents to be:
- Understandable
- Readable
- Straightforward
- Natural

Let us consider these in turn.

UNDERSTANDABLE

Clarity has been mentioned already. Its necessity may seem to go without saying, though some of what one sees of prevailing standards suggests the opposite. It is all too easy to find everyday examples of wording that is less than clear; indeed, some have already been quoted. Another favorite is a sign you still see in some stores: "EARS PIERCED, WHILE YOU WAIT." Is there some other way?

Clarity is assisted by many of the elements mentioned in this Step, but three factors help immensely.

- **Using the right words.** For example, are you writing about "recommendations" or "options," about "objectives" (desired results) or "strategies" (routes to achieving objectives), and when do you use "aims" or "goals"?

- **Using the right phrases.** What is "24-hour service" exactly, other than an insufficiently specific description? Ditto "personal service"? Is this just saying it is done by people? If so, it is hardly a glimpse of anything but the obvious; perhaps it needs expanding to explain the nature, and possible excellence, of the particular service approach

- **Selecting and arranging words to ensure your meaning is clear.** For example, saying, "At this stage, the arrangement is ..." implies that later it will be something else, when this might not be intended. Saying, "After working late into the night, the report

will be with you this afternoon" seems to imply
(because of the sequence and arrangement of words)
that it is the report that was working late, rather than
its writer

Even changing a word or two can make a difference.
Saying something is "quite nice" is so bland that it
understates something that is "hugely enjoyable" to the
extent that it is almost insulting.

 Blandness is certainly to be avoided; it
is unlikely to add power to your case.

Choosing the wrong word is another matter: it can
confuse, upset – or worse. The examples below are designed
to show the danger.

Which word to use? Let us start with a couple of simple
everyday words: "comic" and "comical." Mean much the
same thing?

No. Something "comic" is intended to be funny,
whereas something "comical" is funny unintentionally.

More relevant in a business context are the following.

- "Continuous" (unbroken or uninterrupted) is distinct
  from "continual" (repeated or recurring). A project
  might be "continuous" (in process all the time), but
  work on it is more likely to be "continual" (unless you
  never sleep)
- "Loath," as in being "loath to do something," means
  reluctant; to "loathe" is to hate

- Are you "uninterested" in a proposal, or "disinterested" in it? The first implies you are apathetic, and care not either way; the latter means you have nothing to gain from it
- "Dissatisfied" and "unsatisfied" should not be confused. The first means disappointed; the second means needing more of something
- You might want something to be "expeditious" (quick and efficient), but saying it is "expedient" might not be so well regarded, as it means only that something is convenient (not always a good reason to do anything)
- "Fortuitous" implies something happening accidentally; it is not the same as "fortunate"
- If you are a "practical" person, then you are effective; if something is "practicable," it is merely possible to do; if something is "pragmatic," it is meant, but not proven, to be effective

One wrong word may do damage, but a number of wrong words quickly create nonsense: "This practicable approach will ensure the project is continual. It is fortuitous that I am uninterested in it, and I am sure I will not be unsatisfied to see it start."

Of course, no inaccurate use of language will help you put a message over well, even if it only annoys rather than confuses. For example, saying "imply" when you mean "infer"; writing "12 noon" when "noon" tells you everything you need to know; or talking about an "ATM machine" when the "M" stands for machine (a machine machine?).

Some care, perhaps even some consultation of a dictionary, may be useful.

READABLE
Readability is difficult to define, but we all know it when we experience it. Your writing must flow. One point must lead to another; the writing must strike the right tone and inject a little variety; and, above all, there must be a logical, and visible, structure to carry the message along. As well as the shape, which was discussed earlier, the technique of "signposting" (flagging what is to come) helps the reader, in a practical sense, to understand where something is going and to find their way through easily. It makes them read on, content that the direction is sensible. Signposting is difficult to overuse, and it can be utilized at several levels within the text.

STRAIGHTFORWARD
This means simple to understand. Follow the well-known acronym KISS (keep it simple, stupid).

A series of approaches, each straightforward to keep in mind, can keep what you write straightforwardly presented. Use the following.

- **Short words.** Why "elucidate" something when you can "explain"? Why say "reimbursements" rather than "expenses"? Similarly, although "experiment" and "test" do have slightly different meanings, in a general sense "test" may be better; or you could use "try." The Americans have a good way of putting this:

do not use 50-cent words to make 5-cent points. I always remember what Mark Twain said: "I never write 'metropolis' for seven cents because I can get the same money for 'city'."

- **Short phrases.** Do not say "at this moment in time" when you mean "now," or "respectfully acknowledge" something, a suggestion perhaps, when you can simply say "thank you for"

- **Short sentences.** Having too many overlong sentences is a frequent characteristic of poor business documents. Short sentences are good. However, they should be mixed in with longer ones, or reading becomes rather like the action of a machine gun. Many reports contain sentences that are overlong, often because they mix two rather different points. Break these into two sentences, and the overall readability improves

- **Short paragraphs.** If there are plenty of headings and bullet points, it may be difficult to get this wrong, but keep an eye on it. Regular and appropriate breaks, as the message builds up, do contribute to making reading easy

NATURAL

Some people write in an unnatural fashion. Such a style may just be old-fashioned or bureaucratic. However, it could be made worse by attempts to create self-importance, or to make a topic seem weightier than it is. Just a few words can change the tone: saying "the writer" may easily sound pompous, especially if there is no reason not to say "I."

Business documents do need some formality, but they are, after all, an alternative to talking to people. They should be as close to speech as is reasonably possible. It is not suggested that you overdo this, either by becoming too chatty or by writing "won't" (which you might acceptably say), when "will not" is genuinely more suitable. However, if you compose what you write much as you would say it, and then tighten it up a little, the end result is often better than when you set out to create something that is "formal business writing."

The problem of an artificial style is compounded these days by the sending of overly abbreviated text and email messages. I am all for saving time, but not at the expense of diluting clarity.

! ● **Most business communications should maintain a greater degree of formality than you see in a text message, and while abbreviations have their uses, when to use them needs judicious consideration.**

Readers' dislikes

Readers also hope that what they read will *not* be:

- **Introspective.** It is appropriate in most business documents to use the word "you" more than "I" (or "we," "the company," "the department," and so on). Thus, "I will circulate more detailed information soon" might be better phrased as, "You will receive more detailed information (from me) soon." More so, perhaps, if you add a phrase like "so that you can judge for yourselves." This approach is especially important if there is persuasion involved

- **Condescending**. "As an expert, I can tell you this must be avoided. You must never ..." Bad start – it sounds condescending. You are only likely to carry people with you if you avoid this kind of thing. As an educational broadcast on radio put it: "Never talk down to people, never be condescending. You do know what 'condescending' means, don't you?" Enough said

- **Biased.** Or rather, readers hope that they will detect no bias where it is not intended. A manager writing something to staff setting out why they think something is a good idea, and then asking for their staff's views, may prompt more agreement than is actually felt. If views are wanted, then it is better simply to set something out and ask for comment, without expressing a positive personal view in advance

- **Politically incorrect.** There is a considerable sensitivity about political correctness, which should neither be ignored nor underestimated. As there is still no word that means "he/she," some contrivance may occasionally be necessary in this respect. Similarly, choice of words needs care. One might be pulled up these days for using the expression "manning the office." If you meant who was on duty at a particular time, rather than anything to do with recruitment or selection (which the usually suggested alternative of "staffing" seems to imply), this might seem somewhat silly. But if it matters, it matters; while the way you write should not become labored so to accommodate such matters, some care is certainly necessary

There is a considerable amount to bear in mind here. The focus must be on the reader throughout. However, you must not forget your own position as the writer; there are things here also that must be incorporated into the way you write.

The writer's approach

Every organization has an image. The only question is whether this just happens, for good or ill, or if it is seen as something that should be actively created, maintained, and made positive. Similarly, every memo, report, or proposal you write says something about you. Whether you like it or not, this is true. And it matters. The profile wittingly or unwittingly presented may influence whether people believe, trust, or like you. It may influence how they feel about your expertise, or whether they can see themselves agreeing with you or doing business with you.

Your personal profile is not only an influence in your job, one that links to the objectives you have, it also potentially affects your career. Given the profusion of paperwork in most organizations, it is unavoidable that what you write progressively typecasts you in the eyes of others – including your boss – as the sort of person who is going places, or not.

Certainly, your prevailing style, and what a particular

document says about you, is worth thinking about. If there is an inevitable subtext of this sort, you cannot afford to let it go by default; you need to consciously influence it. Start by considering what you want people to think of you. Take a simple point: you want to be thought of as efficient. The style of the document surely says something about this. If the writing is good, contains everything the reader wants, and covers everything it said it would, then a sense of efficiency will follow. The same applies to many characteristics: being seen as knowledgeable, experienced, authoritative, and so on. It is worth considering how you can achieve the effect you want with all such characteristics.

! **Images are cumulative. They build up over time, and can assist in the establishment and maintenance of relationships.**

Whether you are concerned with relating to a colleague or customer, or with proving to the boss that you are a good person to work with (as well as good at your work), the influence of your image can be powerful.

Similarly, you might have in mind a list of characteristics that you want to avoid seeming to embrace. For example, appearing dogmatic, patronizing, inflexible, or old-fashioned in your job might do you little good. Other characteristics are sometimes to be emphasized, sometimes not. Stubbornness is a good case in point.

Images are not created in a word. There is more to

appearing honest than writing, "Let me be completely honest" (which might actually just ring alarm bells!). Your intended profile will come, in part, from specifics such as choice of words, but also from the whole way in which you use language. So we now turn to more about the use of language.

THE USE OF LANGUAGE

How language is used makes a difference to exactly how a message is received. The importance of using the right word has already been touched on, but the kind of difference we are talking about can be well demonstrated by changing no more than one word. For example, consider the first sentence after the last heading: "How language is used makes a difference to exactly how a message is received." Add one word: "How language is used makes a *big* difference to exactly how a message is received."

Now let us see the effect that changing the word "big" makes. It is surely a little different to say, "How language is used makes a *great* difference to exactly how a message is received." There are many alternatives, all with varying meaning: "real," "powerful," "considerable," "vast," "large," "significant." You can doubtless think of more. In the context of what I am actually saying here, "powerful" is a good word. It is not just a question of how you use language, but what you achieve by your use of it.

(Note: no good business writer should be without a dictionary and thesaurus beside their desk; the latter is often the most useful.)

Making language work for you

Often business writing is almost wholly without adjectives.

Yet, surely, one of the first purposes of language is to be *descriptive*. Most writing necessitates the need to paint a picture, to some degree at least. Contrast two phrases:

smooth as silk
sort of shiny

The first (used as a slogan by Thai Airways) conjures up a clear and precise picture. The second might mean almost anything; dead wet fish are "sort of shiny," but they are hardly to be compared with the touch of silk. An even more descriptive phrase may be required: What about "slippery as a freshly buttered ice rink" (a phrase I heard on the radio)? Could anyone think this means anything other than *really* slippery?

The question of expecting writing to be complex (or to have a high cognitive cost) was mentioned earlier. To some extent, it does not matter whether a document is short or long, if it makes things effortlessly clear. If it is descriptive as well as making something easy to understand, then it is appreciated all the more by readers.

Clear description may need working at, but the effort is worth while. Trainers often ask a meeting venue to be set up for a seminar, in which a group is arranged "in a U shape." You can put people in a U around a single, boardroom-style table. But, more often, it means a U in the sense of an open U, one that gives the trainer the ability to stand within the U to work with individual delegates. Two different layouts, which both demand precise description.

Description is important, but sometimes we want more than that. We want writing to be *memorable* as well as descriptive. This is achieved in two ways: first, by language that is descriptive yet unusual; and second, by language that is descriptive and unexpected.

Returning to the venue theme above, a conference executive who, in explaining the layout of rooms, describes a U shape as "an arrangement that puts everyone in the front row" is using language that is both descriptive and memorable, because while the description is clear and apt, it is also unusual and unexpected. Such phrases work well and are worth searching for.

As another example of the two ways of being memorable, consider a description I once put in a report. In summarizing a perception survey (researching the views customers and contacts held of a client organization), I wanted to describe the view of the majority of people. They liked the organization, were well disposed toward using it, but also found it a little bureaucratic, slow, and less efficient and innovative than they would have wished. I wrote that the organization was seen as "being a bit like a comfortable, but run-down and threadbare old sofa, when people wanted it to be like a modern, leather executive chair." This is clearly descriptive, but gained from being not only unusual, but also not the kind of phrase that is typically used in business writing. Its being memorable was confirmed, because at subsequent meetings it was used by the organization's own people to describe the changes that the report had highlighted as necessary.

There are occasions when this kind of approach works well, not least in ensuring that something about the writer is expressed along the way. Some phrases or passages may draw strength, because the reader would never feel it was quite appropriate to put it like that themselves, yet find they like reading it.

Another aspect you may want, on occasion, to put into your writing is emotion. If you want to seem enthusiastic, interested, surprised – whatever – this must show. A dead, passive style ("The results were not quite as expected; they showed that ...") is not the same as one that characterizes what is said with emotion ("You will be surprised by the results, which showed that ..."). Both may be appropriate in different circumstances, but the latter might be strengthened still further ("The results will amaze ...").

Consider this. How often, when you are searching for the right phrase, do you reject something as either not sufficiently formal or not sufficiently conventional? Be honest. Many are on the brink of putting down something that will be memorable or will add power, and then they play safe and opt for something else. What you select may be adequate, but if it fails to impress, then it may well represent a lost opportunity.

Next, we look at some things to avoid.

Mistakes to avoid

Some things may act to dilute the power of your writing. They may, or may not, be technically wrong, but they end up reducing your effectiveness and making your objectives less certain to be achieved. Here are some examples.

BLANDNESS

Watch out! This is a regular trap for the business writer. It happens not so much because you choose the wrong thing to write, but because you are writing on automatic pilot, without thought – or, at least, without much thought – for the detail, and so you make no real conscious choice.

What does it mean to say something is:

quite good/bad?

rather expensive?

very slow progress?

What exactly is:

an *attractive* promotion? (as opposed to a "profit-generating" one, perhaps)

a *slight* delay? (for a moment/for a month?)

All such phrases give only a vague impression. Ask yourself exactly what you want to express, then choose language that does just that.

"OFFICE-SPEAK"

This is another all-too-common component of some business writing, much of it passed on from one person to another without comment or change. It may confuse little, but adds little either – other than a worn-out, or excessively formal, feel.

Phrases such as these should be avoided:

enclosed *for your perusal* (surely very old-fashioned; even "enclosed *for your interest*" may be unsuitable – you may better tell the other person why the enclosure should be of interest, or simply use "enclosed" alone)

we respectfully acknowledge receipt of (why not say "thank you for"?)

in the event that ("if" is surely better)

very high-speed operation (use "*fast* operation," or state how fast)

the market was *conceptualized* as rigid (try "the market was *considered* rigid")

! ● Avoid trite expressions scrupulously, and work to change the habit of any pet phrases you use all too easily, all too often, and inappropriately.

LANGUAGE OF "FASHION"

Language is changing all the time. New words and phrases enter the language almost daily, often from other countries and/or linked to the use of technology. It is worth watching for the life cycle of such words and phrases, because if you are out of step, then they may fail to do the job you want. I notice three stages:

1. When it is too early to use the words and phrases –

when they will either not be understood, or seem silly
and like failed attempts at trendiness.
2. When the words and phrases work well and don't jar
or draw attention to themselves.
3. When a word or expression begins to date, and sound
wrong or inadequate.

Examples may date, too, but let me try. When a UK
radio program talks about an "upcoming" event, for some
people this word is at the first stage, and does not sound right
at all; "forthcoming" will suit me well for a while longer.

On the other hand, what did we say before we said
"mission statement"? This is certainly a term in current use,
or at the second stage. Most people in business appreciate
its meaning, and some have made good use of the thinking
that goes into producing a mission statement.

What about a word or phrase that is past its best, or
at the third stage? To suggest a common one, what about
"user-friendly"? When first employed, this expression was
new and nicely descriptive, and quickly became handy.
Now, with no gadget on the entire planet not so described
by its makers, the term is becoming somewhat weak, to say
the least.

PET HATES

Some errors are actually well known to most people, yet they
still slip through, and there is a category that simply shares
the fact that many people find them annoying when they
are on the receiving end. A simple example is the adjective

"unique," which is so often used with an adverb. "Unique" means something is like nothing else. Nothing can be "*very* unique" or "*greatly* unique," even the company whose brochure I saw with the words "very unique" occurring three times in one paragraph. So, do not have a product that is more than just unique, even once. Think of similar examples that annoy you, and avoid them, too.

Others here include the likes of:

different to (use "different from" instead)

less (which relates to quantity, used when numbers are involved, where "fewer" would be correct)

Another area for care is with unnecessary apostrophe's [sic], which are becoming a modern plague, and continue unabated, even after so many of us have read Lynne Truss's wonderful book *Eats, Shoots & Leaves* (Profile Books, 2003).

Note, too, that those in any specialist field run the risk of using their own jargon and technical phrases, forgetting that they may not be understood by others. So, for example, a hotel should not talk about "covers" (place settings at a restaurant table) or "provisional reservations" without explaining them. (The latter may be interpreted very differently by different hotels.)

CLICHÉS

This is a somewhat difficult area. Any overused phrase can become categorized as a cliché. Yet a phrase like "putting the cart before the horse" is not only well known, but establishes an instant and precise vision – and can therefore be useful. In a sense, people like to conjure up a familiar image, and so such phrases should not always be avoided, and reports may not be the place for creative alternatives like "spread the butter before the jam." Clichés should certainly not be overused, and it may be better to make it a rule to avoid them like the plague [*sic*].

Following the rules

What about grammar, syntax, and punctuation? Of course, they matter; so does spelling, but spell-checkers largely make up for any inadequacies in that area these days. But, as has been said, you need to check carefully, as there are plenty of possibilities for error. However, some of the rules are made to be broken, and some of the old rules are no longer regarded as rules, certainly not for business writing.

Even so, certain things can jar, such as the following.

- **Poor punctuation.** Material with too little punctuation is exhausting to read, especially when coupled with long sentences. Material with too much punctuation can seem awkward and affected. Certain rules do matter here, but the simplest guide is probably breathing. We learn to punctuate speech long before we write anything, so in writing, all that is really necessary is a conscious acknowledgment of pauses. The length of pause, and the nature of what is being said, will indicate the likely solution. In some ways, it is better to have too much punctuation than not enough

- **Tautology** (unnecessary repetition). The classic

example is people who say, "I, myself, personally."
This is to be avoided. Do not "export overseas";
simply "export." Do not "do some forward planning";
simply "plan"

- **Oxymoron** (a word combination that is
  contradictory). This may sound silly – "distinctly
  foggy" – or be a current good way of expressing
  something – "deafening silence." Some sentences can
  cause similar problems of contradiction – "I never
  make predictions; and I never will."

Other things are still regarded as rules by purists, but
work well in business writing, and are now in current use.
A good example here is the rule stating that you should
never begin a sentence with the words "and" or "but." But
you can. And it helps produce tighter writing and avoids
overlong sentences. But ... , or rather however, it also makes
another point; do not overuse this sort of thing.

Another similar rule is that sentences cannot be ended
with prepositions. Yet, "He is a person worth talking to"
really does sound easier on the ear than, "He is a person with
whom it is worth talking." Winston Churchill, on reading a
sentence that injudiciously avoided a prepositional ending,
is said to have commented in the margin: "This is the sort
of English up with which I will not put."

Still other rules may be broken only occasionally. Many
of us have been brought up never to split infinitives, and it
thus comes under the annoyance category most of the time.
There are exceptions, however. Would the most famous one

in the world, *Star Trek*'s "to boldly go where no man has gone before," really be better as "to go boldly where no man has gone before"? I do not think so.

Personal style

Finally, most people have or develop a way of writing that includes things they simply like. Why not, indeed? For example, although the rule books now say they are simply alternatives, some people think that "First, ... Secondly, ... Thirdly, ..." have much more elegance than beginning "Firstly". The reason why matters less than achieving an effect you feel is right.

It would be a duller world if we all did everything the same way, and writing is no exception. There is no harm in using some things for no better reason than that you like them. It is likely to add variety to your writing, and to make it seem distinctively different from that of other people, which may itself be useful.

Certainly, you should always be happy that what you write sounds right. So, to quote the writer Keith Waterhouse, "If, after all this advice, a sentence still reads awkwardly, then what you have there is an awkward sentence. Demolish it and start again."

The nature of a specific document, what it is intended to do, and to whom it is communicating, affects all of this, so we investigate this further in Step 4.

SUMMARY

Overall, remember to:

- Make sure that what you write is not only readable, but designed for your readers
- Put clarity first – understanding is the foundation of good business writing
- Influence the subtext that provides an image of you, and ensure it works as you want
- Make language work for you – be descriptive *and* memorable
- Make your writing correct, but also individual

04

Some Different Forms of Written Communication

> 66 I love being a writer. What I can't stand is the paperwork. 99
>
> *Peter De Vries*

Any written business document must stand up to analysis, and its only real test is whether the reader finds it does the job it was intended to do. This means the document must have a clear purpose, and that what it says, and how it says it, is understandable; and, indeed, that it exhibits any other characteristic that it needs to meet its specific purpose.

This Step acts as a sort of appendix to the last two; in it, we look at the approach necessary for different types of document.

At this point, it should be noted that there is no one right way to write anything. A variety of styles and of word combinations can be appropriate, but there are some things that must be done in particular ways, and there are certainly things to avoid.

BUSINESS LETTERS

It is easiest to analyze writing through an example, so we start with a typical business letter. This is something that many of us have received, usually addressed by name and slipped under the door to greet us as we rise, on the last day of a stay in a hotel. The example that follows is a real one, though the originator's identifying details (the names of a downtown hotel and its front-office manager) have been removed.

Read the letter on the following page. What are we to make of such a thing? It is a standard letter, used many times each day. This example came to my notice when it was put under my door, and, taking note of the bit about late checkouts ("will be happy to assist you"), I went to the front desk to take advantage. I was told, "Sorry, we're too full to do that today," as were a dozen other people during the ten minutes I stood at the desk. So the first thing to say is that the letter is so badly expressed that it does more harm than good, causing as much disappointment as satisfaction, because it says clearly that something *will happen* when really it may only be *possible*.

Dear Guest,

We would like to thank you for allowing us to serve you here at the – – Hotel, and hope that you are enjoying your stay.

Our records show that you are scheduled to depart today, and we wish to point out that our checkout time is 12 noon. Should you be departing on a later flight, please contact our front-desk associates, who will be happy to assist you with a late checkout. Also, please let us know if you require transportation to the

> airport, so that we can reserve one of our luxury Mercedes limousines.
>
> In order to facilitate your checkout for today, we would like to take this opportunity to present you with a copy of your updated charges, so that you may review them at your convenience. Should you find any irregularities or have any questions regarding the attached charges, please do not hesitate to contact us.
>
> We wish you a pleasant onward journey today, and hope to have the privilege of welcoming you back to the hotel again in the near future.
>
> Yours sincerely,
> (Signature)
> (Name)
> Front-office manager

The letter is also very old-fashioned, with rather pompous-sounding phrases such as "we wish to point out that" and "we would like to take this opportunity," when something shorter, more straightforward, and more businesslike would surely be better.

It almost suggests that the account may be wrong (mentioning "irregularities"), and everything is expressed from an introspective point of view (with "we" leading into five points). No, the letter is no good, and your own analysis may well run to greater length.

The key problem is, perhaps, one of intention. Is the letter designed to:

- Remind people to pay the bill?
- Make checkout quicker or easier?
- Sell a transportation service to the airport?
- Persuade people to come and stay again? (and thus, presumably, give an impression of efficiency and good service)
- Say thank you?

Because it mixes up all of these, to some extent, it fails to do justice to any of them. For example, nothing about the checkout procedure is explained, nor are reasons given as to why someone should stay again. Yet this is surely a straightforward letter; perhaps that is why it was given inadequate thought.

Let us look at another example of a routine business letter: a letter from a training manager to someone who failed to attend a course on the date when they had reserved a place, and who wrote requesting a refund.

For such a thing, sounding too formal or adopting an offhand approach, maybe because of urgency or lack of thought, can create letters that do more harm than good, as with the first letter that follows:

Peter Smith
Clocktower Engineering Limited
Arlton Road
London N1
March 15, 2010

Dear Mr. Smith,

Thank you for your letter of March 14. You will see that you missed attending our training program "Making successful presentations," which you were registered to attend on March 10, because you misread the joining instructions.

The enclosed copy clearly shows that the correct details of time and place were sent to you.

If you want to try again, the program runs again on April 2 this year, at the same venue. You will need to record your intention to attend in writing.

Yours sincerely,
(Signature)
(Name)
Training manager

This is neither polite, helpful, nor likely to win friends and influence people. How about something along the following lines?

Peter Smith
Clocktower Engineering Limited
Arlton Road
London N1
March 15, 2010

Dear Mr. Smith,

Seminar reservation for March 10: "Making successful presentations"

You must have been annoyed to miss attending the above seminar, for which you were registered as a delegate; I was sorry to receive your letter of March 14 setting out the circumstances. In view of the short notice at which you intended to attend, while the joining instructions (copy enclosed) sent to you did give the correct information, we perhaps should have made the details clearer. My apologies.

Luckily the training program is scheduled to run again before too long. I have therefore moved your registration forward to the next date – April 2. The program is running at the same venue.

I hope you will find this convenient, and be able to put the date on your calendar now, while places remain available. Information about this (and about later dates, just in case) is enclosed.

My secretary will phone you in a day or two to check this suits.

I am sure you will find the program useful when you do attend. If you have any special objectives in

attending, do let us know; we aim to meet participants'
needs as I am sure you will find the program useful
when you do attend. If you have any special objectives
in attending, do let us know; we aim to meet
participants' needs as individually as possible.

   I look forward to meeting you next month.

Yours sincerely,
(Signature)
(Name)
Training manager

Better? I think so. Though this example relates only to
a simple confusion (by the client), the approach used in
the second letter, in which the customer is let down gently
and offered convenient alternative action, is preferable. The
difference between the two letters is clear.

SALES LETTERS

Often a document has a very specific purpose, and it must
use the way it is written to achieve that aim. Again, we
examine an example, this time of persuasive (sales) letters.
The example is a letter to a customer, but similar principles
apply whenever persuasion is necessary.

   Sales letters, those specifically designed to be persuasive
rather than just administratively efficient, are a key element
of written communication with customers. Whatever their
purpose, all sales letters must have a clear structure, use
language to make what they say interesting and customer-

oriented, and aim to be persuasive (though the full techniques are beyond the scope of this book).

The letter that follows is responding to an inquiry. The intention here must be clear. You cannot write a letter, or the greater part of it, and then decide how to finish it off and what action to request from the customer. Logically, you must decide what action you want, and then write a letter that is designed to prompt it.

Consider the following, a letter received following a telephone conversation I had with an events manager about the possibility of conducting a training seminar at a hotel on a particular date. Their quoted cost and identifying details are omitted.

Dear Mr. Forsyth,

Following my telephone call with you of yesterday I was delighted to hear of your interest in the – – Hotel for a proposed meeting and luncheon some time in the future.

I have pleasure in enclosing for your perusal our banqueting brochure together with the room plan and, as you can see, some of our rooms could prove most ideal for your requirements.

At this stage, I would be more than happy to offer you our delegate rate of – – to include the following:

- Morning coffee with cookies
- Three-course luncheon with coffee
- Afternoon tea with cookies

- Flip chart, pads, and pencils
- Room rental and visual-aid equipment
- Service and tax

I trust this meets with your approval.

Should you at any time wish to visit our facilities and discuss your particular requirements further, please do not hesitate to contact me but, in the meantime, if you have any queries about the above, I would be very pleased to answer them.

Yours sincerely,
(Signature)
(Name)
Events manager

Let us consider this sales letter for a moment. It is sadly not so untypical in style. Yet, while no doubt well intentioned and polite, and containing a certain amount of information, it does not really begin to *sell* in an appropriate manner. Nor does it project a useful image.

Let us look at the letter again, from the beginning.

- The letter links to the inquiry, but has a weak formulaic start, and no heading. The inquirer does not want to know about the manager's delight (whether or not the latter wants the business). It would be better to start the letter with something about the (potential) client

- The inquirer is not running a "meeting and luncheon"; he had inquired about running a training session. The former is the manager's terminology, not the client's

- The event is not at "some time in the future"; the inquirer had specified a date. The phrasing highlighted here, and in the point above, tells us that the letter is, in all likelihood, a standard one

- Next, we have more of the manager's pleasure. However, the client will be more interested in what the brochure can do for them, than in how it makes the sender feel. (People really do use words like "perusal" in writing, though it seems very old-fashioned to most people. Who would *say* it, though?)

- The term "banqueting brochure" is jargon – the manager's terminology again. (The brochure and room plan may well be useful, nonetheless.)

- Does the hotel have a suitable room or not? The words "some of our rooms could ..." are unclear

- The section about costs starts with the words "At this stage." But I am sure the manager does not mean to say, "We will negotiate later." The phrase is padding, akin to people who start every sentence with the word "Basically"

- Most will find the list all right, but is it fair to assume that it "meets with" the client's "approval"?

- People who use hotels nearly always want to see something like a seminar room in advance, so the manager would be better to assume that, and to make this straightforward to arrange. Also, the manager might better have maintained the initiative, and said they would get in touch. (They never did, incidentally.)

- Expecting the client to "have any queries" seems inappropriate. Is the writer suggesting the letter is inadequate? Anticipating that the client might "seek any additional information" would be more apt

- The further expressions of the manager's delight and pleasure ("I would be more than happy ..." and "I would be very pleased ...") are equally fulsome. The manager is effectively genuflecting to the client, when there are other things that might be more usefully said. All these remarks really say is a rather desperate-sounding "I would love to get your business"

You may find other matters in the letter to comment on, such as the sparse punctuation and overlong sentences. Certainly the net effect does not stand up to any sort of analysis, bearing in mind that the letter's intention is to impress a potential customer.

So how might it be better done? An alternative (and there is, of course, no such thing as a single "correct" version) is shown on the following page:

Dear Mr. Forsyth,

Training seminar: A venue to make your session work well

Your training seminar would, I am sure, go well here. Let me explain why. From how you describe the event, you need a businesslike atmosphere, no distractions, all the necessary equipment, and everything to run like clockwork.

Our seminar room is among a number regularly used for this kind of session, with great success. It is currently free on the days you mentioned: June 3-4. As an example, here is one package that suits many organizers:

- Morning tea/coffee with cookies
- Three-course lunch with tea/coffee
- Afternoon tea/coffee with cookies
- Pads, pencils, and name cards for each participant
- Room rental, with the use of a flip chart and overhead projector

This package costs (sum) per head, inclusive of service and tax. Alternatively, I would be pleased to discuss other options. We aim to meet your specific needs and get every detail just right.

You will almost certainly want to see the room I am suggesting;

I will phone you to set up a convenient time for you to visit. Meantime, our events brochure is enclosed. (You will see the seminar room on page 4.) This, and the room plan with it, will enable you to begin to arrange how your session can work here.

Thank you for thinking of us; I look forward to speaking with you again soon.

Yours sincerely,
(Signature)
(Name)
Events manager

This is much more customer-oriented. The letter has a heading. It starts with a statement that almost any course organizer would identify with: one that indicates, not least, that the writer understands the organizer's point of view (and the word "Your" is upfront). The language of the letter is much more businesslike, and yet closer to what someone would say, the latter helped by expressions like "get every detail just right." (Even omitting the word "just" makes it read less well.) The writer takes the initiative, setting the scene for follow-up action, while making that sound helpful to the customer, and recognizing that they are likely to want to inspect the hotel. Finally, the letter remains courteous; putting a single thank you at the end makes it stand out, and allows for a much less formulaic beginning.

REPORTS

Here, I want to say something about longer documents, in particular reports. First, the greater the length and complexity, the more important it is to prepare carefully: to set clear objectives and focus appropriately on the reader. Secondly (and details will not be repeated again), the length and complexity demand a clear structure.

The simplest structure one can imagine is a beginning, a middle, and an end. (The exact role of these three parts is covered in the context of presentations in Step 5.) Indeed, this arrangement is what a report must consist of, but the argument or case it presents may be somewhat more complex. For example, this may fall naturally into four parts:

1. Setting out the situation.
2. Describing the implications.
3. Reviewing the possibilities.
4. Making recommendations.

The various parts can coexist comfortably; the overriding considerations are logic and organization.

An example helps spell out the logical way in which an argument needs to be presented if it is to be conveyed clearly. Imagine an organization with certain communication problems. A report aimed at correcting these might follow this broad sequence:

1. The situation. This might refer to both the quantity and importance of written communication inside and outside the organization. The situation might also be one of poor writing skills, a lack of standards, or an absence of any training to develop skills or to link them to models recognized within the organization.

2. The implications. These might range from a loss of productivity (because documents take too long to create, and constantly have to be referred back for clarification) to inefficiencies, or worse, resulting from misunderstood communications. The implications could also include damage to image, because of poor documents circulating outside the organization.

3. The possibilities. There might be many possible courses of action, all with their own mix of pros and cons. These might range from limiting report-writing to a small core group of people, through reducing paperwork completely, to setting up a training program and subsequent monitoring system to ensure some improvement takes place.

4. The recommendations. The best options need to be set out. Recommendations need to be specific, addressing exactly what should be done, by whom, and when, alongside such details as cost and logistics chapter.

!● At all stages, generalizations should be avoided. Reports should contain facts, evidence, and sufficient "chapter and verse" for their readers to see them as an appropriate basis for decision or action.

With the overall shape of the argument clearly in mind, you can look in more detail at the shape of the report itself. The way in which it flows from beginning to end is intended to carry the argument, make it easy to follow and read, and render it interesting, as necessary, along the way.

Two special features of reports are useful: appendices and executive summaries. An appendix removes material from the main text, and places it at the end. This allows the main text to be read without distraction, but also allows readers to check details as they wish. An executive summary is a summary in a conventional sense, but unlike a conventional summary, which is put at the end, is put at the beginning, in order to provide an overview of what follows. Essentially, the executive summary acts to say, "What follows is worth reading."

Finally, a report must look right. It needs adequate space, as well as clear headings, numbering, and emphasis (the latter delivered by the use of special typefaces, such as *italic* and **bold**, and assorted graphic devices, such as bullet points).

PRESS RELEASES

Certain documents need a special approach, because of the way they are regarded within the business world and how they are usually experienced. Where a particular format exists, it is worth following carefully, especially when the format is dictated by the recipients of the document.

As an example of a kind of writing that needs to be undertaken with particular precision, we turn to an important element of communications with the media, namely, press releases. These are written communications designed to prompt a mention of something that can be described as "news" about an organization in various media.

Press releases demand that certain conventions are observed; at least, editors will pay more attention to press releases that observe the conventions. These conventions are spelled out below, but you should not follow them too slavishly. Remember that an element of creativity is always necessary, and the overriding idea is to ring bells and differentiate a message from others competing for the same space.

There are two, perhaps conflicting, aspects of putting together a press release that will stand a good chance of publication. The first is to comply with the format prescribed by the newspapers, magazines, and other media to whom press releases are sent; the second is to stand out as being of genuine interest from the very large number of press releases received.

We will take the prescribed format first.

- Put the words "Press release", together with the date, at the top of the first page
- Clearly state, "EMBARGO: not to be published before (time) on (date)," if you need an embargo, that is, a request not to publish before a certain date, to ensure that a news item is fresh when it appears. Underline or use capitals for emphasis
- Put a heading at the top of the first page, below the words mentioned above. The heading should not be too long, but it should be long enough to indicate clearly the contents of the press release, or to generate interest in it
- Ensure that the text of the press release is well spaced

out, by using wide margins, reasonable gaps between paragraphs, and so on. These allow editors to make notes on the document

- Put the word "Continued" or similar at the foot of the page, if the press release runs to more than one page. Even breaking a sentence at the end of the page makes it more likely that editors will turn over the page
- Put the word "End" at the foot of the last page, to make it absolutely clear that there is no more text
- Use newspaper style. Short paragraphs. Short sentences. Two short words rather than one long one
- Keep the press release brief, long enough to put over the message, including running to a second page if necessary, but no more
- Make sure the first sentences summarize the total message, as far as possible
- Avoid overt plugging (although that may well be what you are doing). For example, do not mention names right at the beginning
- Try to stick to facts rather than opinions. For instance, it is better to say, "This event is being arranged for all those who are interested in minimizing their tax liability" than, "This event will be of great interest to all those wanting to minimize their tax liability."
- Ensure that quoted opinions are put in quotation marks and ascribed to individuals. You can also attach a photograph of an individual so quoted. Ideally, submit a black-and-white print, and label it clearly, in case it gets separated from the press release

- Do not overdo the use of adjectives, which can jeopardize credibility
- Do not underline words in the text, in order to avoid confusion with the instruction in printing that all underlined words should be italicized
- Separate notes to the editor from the main text of the press release, by enclosing them in footnotes. This will ensure that a note, such as "Photographers will be welcome," does not get printed as part of the story
- State clearly, at the end of the press release, where further information can be found. Give the contact details, including the telephone number, of this source
- Make sure that the press release is neat, well typed, and presentable, and that it lists any enclosures

So how do you make your press release stand out? There are fewer rules here, but two points are certainly worth bearing in mind:
- Do not "cry wolf." Save press releases for when you really have a story. If you send a series of contrived press releases, you run the risk that a good one among them will be ignored
- Make sure the story sounds interesting and, without overdoing things, be enthusiastic about it. If you are not keen, then why should the recipient be?

Finally, before leaving the subject of press releases, consider the example on the following page of a press release sent out by the publisher of this book.

PRESS RELEASE

Have the Markets Gone Mad?
No, Just Human

Basic Instincts
Human Nature and the New Economics
Pete Lunn

Published by Marshall Cavendish
Publication: June 2008 • Price: £19.99 •
ISBN: 978-0-462-09920-0

London 13 May 2008: Human nature is more sophisticated than economists have long assumed. Thousands of generations of trading with each other have given us subtle yet strong economic instincts. Understanding them can alter how you think about the whole range of economic issues, from when to buy a house to what caused the credit crunch.

In **Basic Instincts**, Pete Lunn reveals the fascinating results of studies conducted by a new breed of economist - the behavioural economists.

By observing our behaviour in a range of scenarios, from mundane shopping to life-changing decisions, behavioural economists are uncovering our most basic economic instincts. Far from the selfish, calculating individuals that traditional economics assumes us to be, people are surprisingly trusting and generous, clubbing together to tackle the uncertainties of economic life.

At a time when economic uncertainty dominates the agenda, Basic Instincts offers new thinking about how the economy really works and what might be done to make it work better.

Bringing together economics and psychology, **Basic Instincts** is a groundbreaking and yet accessible book that presents a clear picture of our decision-making and behaviour in a modern economy.

ENDS

About the author
Pete Lunn is a post doctorate fellow at the Economic and Social Research Institute, Dublin. He has an MSc. in Economics and a Ph.D. from the University of London. He is a former journalist with BBC's Newsnight and was the founding editor of Ireland's first specialist talk radio station, NewsTalk 106.

PR Contact
PR Company Name
Email address
Telephone number

Horses for courses

Whatever kind of document you want to write, whether a brief email or a long report or proposal, you must make it work and make your writing fit the chosen format. This means:

- Having clear intentions
- Keeping in mind the required format when you plan the document
- Following any rules/conventions a format may dictate (as with press releases)
- Making language fit the format (for example, being sufficiently succinct if the format demands brevity)

Finally, always read over what you write carefully, run the spell check (but keep an eye on what it may miss: proper names and so on), and do not send it until you are truly satisfied that it does the job you want in every way. The 'Send Later' feature for emails is perhaps one we should all use more often.

WRITING THAT DISPLAYS A CREATIVE TOUCH

As a final thought – and as a plea to approach business writing creatively and innovatively – consider this: sometimes something special is needed to jolt a reader into action. The second and third communications in pursuit of something are perhaps more difficult than the first communication, in that you may feel you have already given it your best shot, and you may wonder, "What can I do next?" Such follow-up communications can:

- Repeat key issues (although a different way must be found to say at least some of the message)
- Serve as reminders (with good contacts, this may be all that is necessary)
- Offer different action (for instance, the first communication to a customer says, "Buy it," but the second says, "Let us show you a sample"), or find some more novel way of continuing the dialogue

The example below illustrates the last of these points. It highlights that sometimes there is little new left to say, just "It's me again," especially if a good proposition has already been made, and the only reason for a lack of confirmation is that the recipient (here, an existing customer) is busy, rather than unconvinced. In which case, the job is to continue to maintain contact, and ultimately to jog the other party into action, while appearing distinctive or memorable in the process.

After writing a short book for a specialist publisher, I was keen to undertake something for them on another topic in the same format. Proposing the idea got a generally good reaction, but no confirmation. I wrote and telephoned a number of times. Nothing positive materialized – always a delay or a put-off. (You may know the feeling!) When a further message needed to be sent, all the conventional possibilities seemed to have been exhausted. Finally,

I composed the following brief message:

Struggling author,
patient, reliable (nonsmoker), seeks commission on business topics. Novel formats preferred, but anything considered within reason. Ideally 100 or so pages, on a topic like sales excellence sounds good; maybe with some illustrations. Delivery of the right quantity of material – on time – guaranteed. Contact me at the above address/ telephone number, or meet on neutral ground, carrying a copy of *Publishing News* and wearing a carnation.

Despite some hesitation on my part, and concern that I might be going a bit too far (after all, I had only met the recipient once), I sent the message. Gratifyingly, the approach was appreciated, and confirmation of a book contract came the next day.

Sometimes, a slightly less conventional approach – and language that seemingly has nothing to do with business writing – works well. Try a little experiment, and see what it can do for you.

SUMMARY

Written communication presents one of the greatest opportunities to shine as a communicator. This is partly because prevailing standards are not so good; many people find writing a chore, and therefore respect anyone who can do it well. Whatever kind of document you must create, always:

- Prepare thoroughly, and set clear objectives, before you put pen to paper
- Write throughout with a focus on the reader
- Use language, consciously, to make what you say powerful

Finally, let us give the last word on writing to an especially prolific author, Isaac Asimov (who wrote nearly 500 books, mainly science and science fiction). Asked what he would do if told he only had six months to live, he answered simply, "Type faster." Clearly he was someone who enjoyed writing. But his reply is also a good example of the power of language. Think how much his response says about the man and his attitude to life, his work, and his readers; and *in just two words*.

> ! ● Whatever the document, care can maximise its effectiveness and help ensure that it fulfils its intention.

05

On Your Feet

"The human brain starts working the moment you are born and never stops until you stand up to speak in public.**"**

Sir George Jessel

Now we move on to the topic of presentations. Often, this goes hand in hand with what we have reviewed so far – you write something up, and must then make a presentation about it. Making a presentation is certainly a career skill. That is, it is not only important as a task that must be done in an increasing number of jobs, but it is also important to how you are perceived, and even to how you get on in your career. Few organizational jobs are guaranteed never to involve you in making presentations; for many people, the making of presentations is a regular necessity.

I once asked a senior executive about the motivation of the participants in a presentation-skills workshop I was about to run for the organization. He replied very simply, "They are all keen to attend – no one gets promoted in this organization unless they can make a good presentation." This is a common enough sentiment these days.

Yet presenting is not everyone's forte. For most people, acquiring abilities in this area does not just happen.

Presenting needs both study and practice; it is, after all, a practical skill.

! ● **Not everyone will be a great orator, but everyone can – and many must – turn in a workmanlike performance if they understand how to go about it.**

So, now, the job is to say something about what makes a good presentation, and how to achieve it. The intention is simple: to help the reader to be able to prepare, quickly and easily, and deliver a better presentation than might be possible without thought. Above all, the aim is that what is done presentationally will achieve its purpose with some real certainty. Reading this will not remove the need for practice, but a sound understanding of the process will ensure that any practice helps develop skills that make a positive difference to what is done "on your feet," and does so promptly.

UNACCUSTOMED AS I AM

How do you feel if you know you have to make a presentation? Confident? Apprehensive? Terrified? If you feel apprehensive, or even terrified, relax – you are normal. Most people share your feelings to some extent.

In fact, psychologists tell us that feelings about presenting or public speaking are almost wholly negative. People's "self-talk" (inner dialogue) before speaking in public typically consists of a catalogue of intimations of disaster. We say to ourselves things like, "I can't do it," "I'm not ready," "The audience will hate it," "I'll dry up," "I won't have sufficient material," "I don't know how to put it," "I'll lose my place," and, at worst, "I'll die."

What is more, if you stand up unprepared and ignorant of how to go about it, your presentation may well be a disaster. But it need not be. With some knowledge, practice, and effort to think it through, there is no reason on earth why you should not make a good job of it. This Step reviews how to go about making presentations, but, before doing so, let us first consider the nature of presentations.

THE NATURE OF PRESENTATIONS

Presentations are important. There can be a great deal hanging on them – a decision, an agreement, a sale – and they can affect financial results and reputations, too. All sorts of things can be involved. You may have to speak:

- At an internal meeting
- Externally, perhaps to distributors or customers
- To a committee or board
- At a conference or business event
- At a social event (anything from a retirement party, or other social event in a business context, to a wedding)

You may have to speak to people you do, or do not, know; to people more senior or junior than yourself; or to those who are younger or older than you. You may have to speak to 10, 20, or 200 people, or more.

All groups, at whatever event, exhibit one similar

characteristic: They judge you by how you present. An example makes this clear. Imagine that you have to announce some policy change. Let us assume it is something eminently sensible, which should be accepted without trouble. But start, "Now ... um ... what I want to say is ... well, that is, basically ... ," and you may be well on the way to getting even the most innocuous message rejected.

It is a fact of life that something poorly presented can be poorly received, despite the sense of its content. People do not think, "What an excellent idea! A shame it was not put over better." They think, "What a rotten presentation! I bet the ideas were rotten, too."

Significant opportunities

As a result, presentations present significant opportunities. If you can do them well (and you can), then you will positively differentiate yourself from others, who, from ignorance or a lack of care, do an undistinguished or poor job.

So motivation should not be in doubt here. There are few business (or career) skills more worth mastering than that of making presentations. Without the requisite skill, you do not just feel exposed; you are exposed. The trouble is that the ground does not mercifully open up and allow you to disappear, along with your embarrassment. It is more likely that the result is much more real: no agreement, no commitment, or the boss saying ominously, "See me afterwards."

There are good reasons for having fears, but usually these can all be overcome or reduced, in order to stop them overpowering your ability to work successfully. It may help to think of things as a balance. On one side, there are things that can, unless dealt with, reduce your ability to make a good presentation. On the other side, there are techniques that positively assist the process. The right attention to both sides improves your capability.

Much of what will be said here is about the positive techniques. But let us first return to, and spell out a little more about, possible difficulties – some of which are inherent to the process – and how to overcome them; if only to get the negative side out of the way first.

Precarious events

We communicate so much, we tend to take it for granted. Indeed, we regard much of communication as easy, and people may well say of a presentation that they know they could so easily go through the content if they were sitting comfortably opposite just one other person.

But even a moment's thought will remind you that communication is not easy; it can be downright difficult, as we explored in Step 1. This means that every tiny detail matters. Presentations, like documents, are inherently fragile. Small differences – an ill-chosen word or phrase, a hesitation, a misplaced emphasis – can all too easily act to dilute the impact sought. I remember once hearing someone start a presentation by referring to his "fragmented organization." This was just a single ill-chosen expression – he meant that the organization was arranged in different sections, each focusing on different things –

but puzzled looks and unnecessary thinking ("What sort of organization?") occurred just when he should have been getting off to a good start, and engaging people's attention.

At least communication problems constitute a tangible factor. If you resolve to take care, your communication will be better, and you are more certain to be understood. You can work at getting this right. Many of the elements reviewed as we continue will assist this process, but what about less tangible fears?

The stuff of nightmares

Whatever you fear will make a presentation more difficult, you will probably find that others think the same. When I ask groups attending workshops about presentations what their worries are, they usually mention similar factors.

The top ten nightmares of presenters are listed below, in no particular order, with some thoughts about overcoming them.

1. **Getting butterflies.** Without *some* apprehension, which can act to focus you on the job in hand, you will probably not do so well. Much of this feeling will fade as you get under way (and knowing this from practice helps), but you can help the process in a number of ways:
   - Take some deep breaths before you start (nerves tend to make you breathe more shallowly, and starve you of oxygen), and remember to breathe as you go along (running out of breath to the point of gasping is a surprisingly common problem)

- Take a sip of water just before you start
- Do not eat a heavy meal before a presentation
- Do not have an empty stomach (or rumbles may join the butterflies)
- Avoid alcohol (except, possibly, in extreme moderation) – it really does not help. At worst, it may persuade you that you can do something you cannot, and make matters worse as the truth dawns

2. **Having a dry mouth.** This is easily cured. Take a sip of water. Never attempt to speak without a glass of water in front of you. Even if you do not touch it, knowing it is there is a comfort. Choose noncarbonated water; fashionable fizzy water can have distracting side effects!

3. **Not knowing what to do with your hands.** The best solution is to give them something to do – hold the lectern or a pencil, make the occasional gesture – then forget about them. Thinking about them as you proceed will make matters worse.

4. **Not knowing how loudly to speak.** Just imagine you are speaking to the furthest person in the room (if they were the only one there, you would have little problem judging it); better still, try it beforehand.

5. **Getting a hostile reception.** The vast majority of groups want a presentation to go well. They are disposed to be on your side. The only thing that is worse than standing on the platform knowing that you are not presenting well is being in the audience. Think about it.

6. **Having too little material.** This can be removed completely as a fear. If your presentation is well prepared (of which more soon), you will *know* you have the right amount.

7. **Having too much material.** The same applies as for point 6. Enough said for the moment.

8. **Losing your place.** As another aspect of preparation (which we will review in detail), your speaker's notes should be organized so that you do not lose your place, and so that you can find your place easily if you do.

9. **Drying up.** Why should this happen? Dry mouth? Take a sip of water. Lose your place? Organize it so that this does not happen. Nerves? Well, some of the factors already mentioned will help; so will preparation. If you do dry up, you will find that it only takes a second to resume: "There was another point here. Ah, yes, the question of ...". The problem here can be psychological; it just *feels* as if you paused forever.

10. **Misjudging the timing.** This is something that speaker's notes can help with specifically.

All that is necessary for such problems or thoughts is a practical response, something that acts to remove or reduce the adverse effect. Addressing every issue this way can reduce fears and distractions and leave your mind a little freer to concentrate on the job in hand. Positive thinking helps, too. Try not to worry. No doom and gloom; it will be more likely to go well if you are sure it will. More so if you work at organizing, so that every factor helps.

> **!** Few people can speak without thought.
> The author Mark Twain said: "It
> usually takes me more than three weeks
> to prepare a good impromptu speech."

Preparation is crucial to success, and it is that to which we turn next, building on what was said in Step 2.

READY, SET, ...

Imagine that you have a presentation to make. If you are reading this at all, then you probably do have examples of what you have to do that you can bear in mind; maybe you have one to be done soon. Few people will simply do nothing about it until the day, and then get up and speak. So what do you do? Let us address some dangers first, so as to lead into what is best practice here. What you might do is think of what you want to say first, then think of what follows – what you will say second, third, and so on – and, after that, write it down word for word. Finally, perhaps after some judicious amendment, you read it to the group you must address.

Wrong, wrong, and wrong again.

Doing so might sound logical, but contains the seeds of disaster. We will pick up some alternative approaches as we continue. As it is a straightforward factor to address, let us take the reading aspect first.

Trying not to read verbatim

Some people think, at least until they have more experience, that having every word down on paper, and reading the words out, acts as a form of security. After all, what can go wrong if you have everything, right down to the last comma, in black and white in front of you? Well, two things in particular.

First, you will find it is very difficult to read anything smoothly, get all the emphasis exactly where it needs to be, and do so fluently and without stumbling. The actors who record novels, and other books, as audio works deserve their paychecks – real skill is involved here. Another modern blight caused by this is apparent in the style of many politicians:

They pause as it were –
Inserting a comma only –
When they come to the end of –
A line on the teleprompter.

This can produce an awkward, and sometimes amusing, effect.

Most people speak very much better from notes that are an abbreviation of what they intend to say. If you doubt this, just try it – read something out loud and see how it sounds; better still, record it and hear how it sounds. In addition, certainly in a business context, you rarely need to be able to guarantee so exact a form of wording. (There are exceptions, of course; a key definition or description may need to be word-perfect.) It is usually more important to ensure that the emphasis, variety, and pace are right; that is what is so difficult to achieve when reading.

Secondly, preparation cannot be done in isolation. It

links to two factors that are vital in making an effective presentation. These are:

- Having clear objectives
- Taking account of your audience

As many would say that the audience is the principal factor here, let us start with that.

Taking account of your audience

Good preparation starts with taking account of your audience. First of all, who are they? They may be people you do, or do not, know; men or women; expert or inexpert about whatever topic you must address. There are many permutations here. Most important, however, are the *audience's* expectations: what do they want?

Put yourself in their place. Faced with listening to a presentation, what do you say to yourself? Most people anticipate its impact on them: "Will this be interesting, useful, long, or short? What will this person be like? Will I want to listen to them? How will what they have to say help me?" Again, the permutations are many (though usually not too complicated to think through), and bearing audience viewpoint in mind is a major factor in ensuring a successful outcome.

Specifically, any audience *wants* you to:

- Know your stuff
- Look the part
- Respect them, that is, acknowledge their situation and views

- Discover links between what you say and what they want from the talk
- Give an adequate message, so that they can understand and weigh up whether they agree with what is said or not (this is especially important if you are going to suggest or demand action of them)
- Tailor the talk to their requirements, for example, in terms of the level of technicality
- Hold their attention and interest throughout

It is equally important to bear in mind what an audience does not want. This includes not being:
- Confused
- Blinded by science, technicalities, or jargon
- Lost in a convoluted or nonexistent structure
- Made to struggle to understand inappropriate language
- Made to stretch to relate what is said to their own circumstances

Nor do they want to listen to someone who, by being ill prepared, shows no respect for the group.

A good presenter will always have empathy for the group they address, and the empathy must be evident to them. Often, this is something guided by prior knowledge. But it can, of course, vary; you may well need to speak to groups you do not know well. Always find out what you can about them, and make use of everything you do discover.

Some of what makes for the right approach here is an amalgam of the various techniques we will explore later;

some relates to immediate practical factors that every presenter would do well to remember. For example, I would not presume to tell you how to dress for a presentation, but it bears thinking about. Professionalism is, at least in part, inferred from appearance. Personal organization has a visual importance, too. You must not just be well organized; you must *look* well organized. Walking to the front of a room, however confidently, is likely to be spoiled if you are clutching a bulging folder spilling papers in all directions, and start by saying, "I am sure I have the first slide here somewhere," accompanied by fevered fumbling attempts to find it.

Having clear objectives

Rarely, if ever, will you be asked just to "talk about" something. The most crucial question any intending presenter can ask themselves is, "Why is this presentation to be made?" If you can answer that, your talk will be easier both to prepare and present.

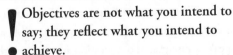

Objectives are not what you intend to say; they reflect what you intend to achieve.

Forgive me if this seems obvious, but I regularly observe presentations (often carefully prepared and brought to training workshops in the knowledge that they will be subject to critique) that are poor almost solely because they have no clear objectives. They rattle along reasonably well, yet they do not *go* anywhere.

The acronym SMART (specific, measurable, achievable, realistic, timed), already discussed in Step 2, serves as a good example of a number of objectives that might be applied when preparing a presentation. You might usefully glance back at the relevant section, "Setting objectives," in Step 2 before reading on.

Drafting your speaker's notes

We have already outlined a systematic approach, in six stages, for putting together a presentation. (See Step 2 for more details.) You may recall that stages 1-4 consisted of listing, sorting, arranging, and reviewing content. At stage 5, your content needs to be turned into speaker's notes, from which you can work easily to deliver your message accurately and with the desired emphasis. At this stage, the focus is not so much on *what* is said as on *how* it is said.

Remember the tips given in Step 2: *choose the right moment* for drafting your speaker's notes, and, once you have started drafting, *keep going*, and try not to pause or be interrupted. These tactics really do make the process easier.

For most people, having *something* in front of them as they speak is essential. The question is what exactly this should be. Speaker's notes have several roles, notably to:

- Boost confidence (in the event, you may not need everything that is in front of you, but knowing that it is there is, in itself, useful)
- Act as a guide to what you will say, and in what order
- Help with saying it in the best possible way, with the right variety, pace, emphasis, and so on, as you go along

On the other hand, your speaker's notes must not act as a straitjacket, stifling all possibility of flexibility. After all, what happens if your audience's interest suggests that a digression, or more detail, might be welcome before proceeding? Or if your audience's level of knowledge is greater than you had thought, and prompts some recasting or abbreviation of what you had planned to say? Or if, as you get up to speak for half an hour, the person in the chair whispers, "Can you keep it to 20 minutes? We're running a bit behind!"? Good notes should assist with these, and other, scenarios.

Here, I will set out some useful rules, as well as some tried-and-tested approaches. But the intention is not that you should follow these slavishly. It is important to find what suits you, so you may want to try some of the approaches mentioned, but to amend or tailor them to fit your kind of presentation as exactly as possible.

One point is worth making at the outset: there are advantages in adopting a consistent approach to how you work here. If you do so, you can be more sure of your preparation, and you are more likely to become quicker at getting your preparation done. A consistent approach also helps you judge how long it will take to present your material.

The following might be adopted as "rules" regarding your speaker's notes.

- **Ensure your notes are legible.** You must use sufficiently large type or handwriting; avoid adding tiny untidy embellishments; and remember that notes must be suitable to be used standing up, and therefore at a greater distance from your eyes than if you were sitting and reading them

- **Choose your materials to suit you.** Some people favor small cards, others larger sheets. A standard A4 (210 * 297mm) ring binder works well. (One with a pocket at the front may be useful for holding items you want with you.) Whatever materials you choose, make sure they *lie flat* – it is certain to be disconcerting if a folded page turns back, especially if you repeat a whole section as a result, as I once saw a speaker do

- **Use one side of the paper only.** This allows for any amendments or additions, and makes your notes easier to follow

- **Number the pages of your notes.** This is a wise precaution. (One day, as sure as the sun rises in the morning, you will drop them!) Some like to number in reverse order – 10, 9, 8, and so on – which gives an idea of the time remaining until the end

- **Use color and symbols.** These will help you find your way, and also minimize what must be noted

At this point, an example may help to clarify how speaker's notes can be used to deliver a presentation successfully. To start with, here is the first part of a short talk on time management:

Good morning! Let's get straight down to business. As you might guess, this is one session that should make a point of starting on time! Indeed, time management is important to everyone.

I am sure we are all busy. Some of us may occasionally feel we have more to do than we can reasonably be expected to cope with – or perhaps "regularly feel" would be a better way of putting it. We may also feel that some of the things we are not getting to are more important, or more interesting, than the jobs bogging us down. And, as one harassed person said to me only a few days ago, "I would just like a moment to think!" It all matters. We will not be effective if everything is always done in a headlong rush.

Today, I want to suggest that we *can* create more time. Who would like five extra minutes? That may not seem much, hardly time to pour a cup of tea, much less do anything useful, but if we save even that much every working day, it is some 30 hours in a year – and which of us could not use roughly four extra days!

Time is a resource, and today I want to help us think about how to maximize its use.

So much is wasted. Interruptions, unnecessary telephone conversations, and seemingly interminable meetings – need I go on? We all know the feeling. What can we do about it? Well, there's good news and bad news.

The bad news is that good time management is difficult, and pressure makes it more so; certainly, getting it right needs conscious effort. But many of the things that make it work are common sense, and good habits can build up surprisingly quickly.

So the good news is that with the right attitude, and with diligent use of some well-applied techniques, we can make a difference – be organized, focus on the priorities, avoid wasting time, and manage the interruptions in a way that minimizes them.

Let's now look at where time goes, then at some of the techniques involved in keeping our work pattern under control.

The wording of this text is pretty much as it might be spoken. Now, here are the speaker's notes that might usefully be in front of the person giving such a talk:

Time: 10 minutes		
It's difficult	GKC " - not tried and found wanting, found difficult and therefore not tried." ! You? _ _ _	OPTIONS
	* Problems - interruptions No magic formula ⟶ * What makes it possible? - Detail - Habit but realistically: never perfect but worthwhile.	e.g. Members of team / lack confidence / always seeking advice

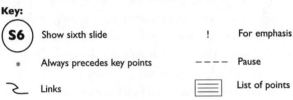

Key:

(S6)	Show sixth slide	!	For emphasis
*	Always precedes key points	– – – –	Pause
↲	Links	▤	List of points

The notes illustrate the quantity and style of guidance you might adopt.

The detail in the speaker's notes needs to be just sufficient for a well-prepared speaker to be able to work from it, and do so comfortably. Consider the devices used in the speaker's notes on the previous page, and, as you do so, try to bear in mind the effect that the use of a second (or third?) color – which cannot be reproduced here – would have on their ease of use. The gray tint represents a highlighter pen. This would be more dramatic in fluorescent yellow, but its use is still clear in black-and-white print.

As for the ideas incorporated into the speaker's notes, there should be things here that you can copy or adapt, or which prompt additional ideas that suit you. The following are used in the example of speaker's notes.

- **Divisions.** The page (which you should imagine as being A4) is divided by a line (which, ideally, should be colored) into smaller segments, each creating a manageable area on which the eye can focus with ease. This helps ensure that you do not lose your place
- **Symbols.** These save space and, visually speaking, jump off the page, making sure you do not miss them. It is best to avoid possible confusion by always using the same symbol to represent the same thing, and maybe also by restricting the number of symbols used
- **Columns.** These separate different elements of the notes. Clearly, there are various options here, in terms of number of columns and what goes where
- **Space.** Turning over a page only takes a second – often, you can end a page where a slight pause is necessary anyway – so you might as well give yourself plenty of space, not least to facilitate amendments and, of course, to allow individual elements to stand out
- **Emphasis.** This must be as clear as content; again, a second color helps
- **Timing.** An indication of time elapsed (or still to go) can be included as little or often as you find useful. Remember that every audience loves to have time commitments kept
- **Options.** These, as a separate element, can be particularly useful. Options can be added or omitted as you go along, depending on such factors as time and feedback. They help fine-tune the final delivery, and are good for your confidence, too.

> **!** Good preparation and good notes
> **●** go together. If you are well prepared,
> confident of your material, and
> confident also that you have a really clear
> guide in front of you, then you are well on
> the way to making a good presentation.

With your speaker's notes drafted, you have now reached stage 6 in the process of putting together your presentation. You may wish to refer back to Step 2 to remind yourself of what to do at this stage.

Rehearsal

Preparation may be defined as including rehearsal, but they are two different things. Rehearsal may be more or less formal, and take more or less time. At one end of the scale is just talking it through in your head (not least to check duration). At the other is getting people to listen to a dry run – though with the intention, perhaps, that it should not be too dry. You can go further, for example, using a sound or video recorder, or organizing a more formal counseling session. The choice is yours, and is dictated by the importance of the event, and the confidence you have in what you can do.

Rehearsal can also sensibly include such things as:
- Checking out the speaking area
- Trying slides to ensure they are legible, especially from the back of the room (incidentally, *never* ask, "Can

you see that OK?" – you should know your audience
can)
- Checking any other equipment that will be used
- Ensuring a clear brief from anyone who will be in the
  chair (it is annoying, to say the least, to find that you
  are interrupted, and the chair invites the group to go
  take a coffee break, when you were only planning to
  speak for perhaps two more minutes – either agreeing
  or explaining during the presentation will destroy
  the flow)

If you are speaking as part of a team, *always* make sure
that speakers get together ahead of the event to rehearse,
or at least discuss, all handovers and any possible overlaps.
You are seeking a seamless transition between individual
contributors.

Some final rules

Throughout the process of preparation, always remember
to:
- Think positive (actively combating that all-too-
  common negative "self-talk" before public speaking)
- Give preparation *sufficient* time (which includes
  starting it early enough and, though sometimes
  difficult to do, organizing time free of interruption)

"Ready, set, go!" is always the best order in which to
proceed. In the next section, we move on to the presenter's
equivalent of "go!"

GO! MAKING THE PRESENTATION

Making the presentation incorporates *what* you do and how you do it. To keep matters manageable, we look at the "mechanics" of how you structure and move through a presentation, and then at the tricks of the trade, which can make it easier to do, and enliven it further for the audience. Keeping an eye on what the audience expects has been mentioned; this continues to be important throughout the process.

Now, the bulk of the presentation is in the middle, so ... wait a minute, what about ending on a high note? ... but first we should consider ... As you see, the need for structure speaks for itself. But it always needs to be clear what it is, or confusion can still reign. Therefore, while making it clear that this section will deal with aspects of the beginning, the middle, and the end, we will start with a useful technique that informs the audience of what is happening.

Signposting

Here is a technique that can help speaker and audience alike. Signposting does just what it says: it points out what is coming. People like to have an overview and to know where they are. Helping them in this respect scores points, and makes an audience feel comfortable, both with themselves and with the presenter. They stop saying, "Where is this going?" and say, "Right, sounds as if it makes sense. What comes next?" And they listen, too.

This technique is an inherent part of the way that a book like this is presented. The next few lines contain another example, in which a manager is introducing a project-review meeting with a short presentation:

> Let's be sure we are all clear what we need to do in the next hour or so. I intend to bring us up to speed on progress; then to call for section heads to add any comments about their respective areas; then to see what new action is necessary to keep us on course to hit the deadline, and what must be done before the next meeting.

This is an overall statement. It might be followed by more signposting:

> Right, let's get up to date. I will comment about what stage we have reached first, then about how costs are working out, then about feedback.

At the next level down, further signposting might follow:

> Turning to costs, we need to think about materials and staff separately. I will start with materials.

Even this level might need subdividing. It is really true to say that you cannot overuse signposting (although it might be a little more spaced out than in the example above).

The value of this technique, in terms of keeping things

organized, is obvious. Indeed, it is likely to be more useful in this respect with long and complex presentations than with something of five minutes on one straightforward topic. This is not to say that any presentation can afford to be disorganized.

As well as aiding structure, signposting is used to flag individual elements, that is, *what is coming*. For example:

"Here's an example of how that works ..." (stating explicitly that an example is coming)

"For instance, ..." (implying that an example is coming)

Sometimes, it may also be useful to signpost *the nature of what is coming*. For example:

"Let me digress for a moment," (making it clear that the next thing said is away from the stated content)

"Now, a key detail ..." (getting the audience ready to concentrate on something important)

"Perhaps I can add something here," (making it clear that the digression is extra to the stated content)

"On a less serious note, ..." (implying an aside that may amuse)

In using this sort of device, it may add to its value if you explain the why of the matter also:

"Here's an example that will link what I've been saying to your day-to-day work."

All this does more than simply inform; it also influences. The choice of words can prompt an audience to pay particular attention, relate what is being said to their situation, make a note, remember something that needs to be in mind alongside what comes next, and so on.

But, we are getting ahead of ourselves. Following a new signpost of my own, we now turn from how to indicate structure to the structure itself: the beginning, the middle, and the end.

In the beginning

It is said that you never get a second chance to make a good first impression. It may be a cliché, but you forget it at your peril. A good start has a positive effect on the audience and on the presenter – it can be a wonderful feeling when, after initial apprehension, you realize you are a couple of minutes in, and all is going well; it boosts your confidence, helping you successfully deliver what is still to come.

It follows logically that the beginning needs especially careful preparation. Your notes for this stage may need to be just a little fuller than for later stages. Thorough preparation is all the more important when you consider the complexity of what needs to be done in the opening.

The beginning is an introduction. It must make clear *why* the presentation is being made. (Remember what was said about objectives earlier in this Step, as well as in Step 2.) The scene must be set, the topic introduced, and the theme stated (and possibly the boundaries drawn – "In the time available, I will highlight what seem to me the key issues ..."). All this must be done clearly.

At the same time, you must aim to have some impact on the audience in two different ways:

- By getting their attention
- By creating a rapport with them

Success with these two factors early on can influence the way the whole presentation goes throughout its duration and thus how it is received. So both factors are important and both deserve an individual word.

GETTING THE AUDIENCE'S ATTENTION

There are two broad ways of starting:
- With the formalities
- With something ahead of the formalities

On some occasions, it may be suitable to say:

> Good morning, ladies and gentlemen. Thank you for the opportunity to talk to you today about presentation skills.

As long as this element is brief, it is seen as being a formality, and the audience goes along with it, expecting something more interesting to come along soon.

The formalities may be important, but they do not have to open a presentation. For example, if a thank you is called for, it should certainly not be omitted, but it does not have to lead. Thus, it may be equally, if not more, suitable to say:

The next 30 minutes will help you do an important job better and more quickly than you do it now. What job? Making presentations. Before saying something about how you can be more effective in this task, let me thank ...

You may find it useful to think of other ways in which you can aim to get the audience's attention. The following list starts the process.

- **Surprise them with something they do not know.** "Hot from the press – the trade-journal feature we have been waiting for is out, and it gives us a real plug. This will ..."

- **Ask them a question.** "How many hours of productivity were wasted last month?" This can be rhetorical, closely followed by "Let me tell you, some ... hours were wasted," or actual, though the latter can lead to early digression if the response is not quite as expected

- **Trigger their curiosity.** "How many of you are afraid of spiders?" In a talk about the art of public speaking, this may seem like an odd beginning, but it prompts an active response, with people saying to themselves, "How does this fit in?" Then, if a link is quickly made with other fears, including the fear of speaking in public, you hold the audience's attention (at least for the moment)

- **Remind them of something** (such as a common experience). "This time last year, when we met at the annual planning meeting, I said ..." Then, lead on from that

- **Give them something to watch.** Exclaim, "Time is running out ... ," accompanied by a gesture, in which you slowly take off your watch (which may, in any case, be more use in front of you) or point to a wall clock
- **Say something designed to be dramatic** (and spoken in a way that matches). "The next half hour can change the organization's fortunes forever. How? By ..."
- **Tell them an anecdote** (possibly with a humorous edge). "Once upon a time ..." But be careful, as humor carries its own risks – for advice on the safe use of humor, see the section "Some humor" later in this Step
- **Appraise them of a fact** (something relevant to the topic). "90% of the telephone support staff are asking for leave in the first part of July, and that is just one reason for reviewing certain staffing policies ..."
- **Quote something** (preferably something relevant, which makes a point). "The physicist Niels Bohr said, 'Predictions can be very difficult – especially about the future.' He had a point. But I must try and do just that."
- **Say nothing.** Well, say something, but then pause. "Listen." (The presenter silently counts to ten.) "Not a sound – isn't *anyone* doing any work around here?"

Such devices can be linked, adapted, or extended, but always the first few words or sentences need actively to seek attention. Often, they may be sensibly combined with some clear signposting of what is to come thereafter.

CREATING A RAPPORT WITH THE AUDIENCE

No one wants to sit through a presentation that is tedious, dull, and irrelevant. If a speaker's "self-talk" beforehand is largely negative, it is probably true to say that members of the audience have primarily positive feelings; at least in the absence of indications that they should take a view to the contrary. They want the presentation to be interesting and successful. They are inclined to give it the benefit of the doubt, and if they warm to you as well as to what you say, this increases the likelihood of overall acceptance.

So there is a need to foster group feeling; this means you must have a clear idea of how you want to be regarded. Remember that you need to decide whether you want to be seen as expert, authoritative, sympathetic – whatever. Such a list of characteristics is not, of course, mutually exclusive; you must match your projected image to the occasion and the audience.

One factor is universally useful – enthusiasm. It is one of the few good things in life that is contagious. It can have a powerful effect. Expressing enthusiasm – and the feeling must be sincere – tends to make you appear more animated, which is also a good thing, and provides a good starting point to the flavor that you want to put across. With few exceptions – even a funeral tribute may need it – enthusiasm should be a standard part of your approach.

Beyond this, there are various other factors that, together or separately, may help you to build a rapport with the audience.

- **Select the appropriate form of address.** Think about
  the difference between the following:

  We should consider ...

  You should consider ...

  I think you should consider ...

  Most people find ... worth considering

  All of these have a different feel to them. Other phraseology
  affects feeling in this sort of way. For example, consider
  the difference between "must do," "should do," "might
  find it useful to do," and so on. Choice here indicates
  your approach, about which people can then form a view.

- **Use a compliment.** Do not overdo it and sound
  patronizing, but you might find it useful to say, "Being
  expert in this area yourselves, you will ... "
- **Link your situation or experience to that of the
  audience.** Use phrases like "We all know the problem
  of ... ," which make it clear you are part of the group,
  rather than standing outside *talking at* it

THE END OF THE BEGINNING

The beginning is, by definition, brief, and must sensibly
be regarded and organized as a suitable proportion of the
whole. It must be a separate entity, yet allow a smooth
transition to the middle, or the meat, of the presentation.
Though short, the early moments of a presentation are
disproportionately important (as is their preparation) and
can influence an audience for good or ill.

Above all, the beginning must fulfill its required functions, and generate the intended response in the audience. Both are worth a word or two.

Fulfilling the required functions

The main functions of the beginning are to:

- Define the topic
- Spell out the objectives
- Explain why something is sensible or necessary
- Describe elements of the structure
- Start in an interesting way, so as to suggest that the remainder of the presentation will also be interesting
- Take the first steps toward satisfying the audience's expectations
- Establish a feeling of relevance to the audience

All these are commonly appropriate. The beginning may also need to fulfill more specific functions, as the occasion dictates. Such functions include encouraging people to keep an open mind; setting the scene for later participation; making clear the level of technicality or detail to be entered into; or describing the point, in terms of experience or background, from which the speaker is starting.

Generating the intended response in the audience

It is also useful to think about – and aim at producing – the feelings that the audience would express, if quizzed, as you move from the beginning to the middle. Would they feel that:

- The presentation is being accurately directed at them?
- Their specific needs are being borne in mind?
- The speaker is engaging, or at least worth listening to?
- They identify and agree with what is said?

If so, then you can move on with confidence, and use a good start as a solid foundation on which to build.

ADMINISTRATIVE MATTERS

A final point worth mentioning concerns administrative matters. It may be important to welcome specific people, notify the audience of break or refreshment arrangements, or tell them about policy regarding smoking. The question is when you should make such administrative points, so that they do not dilute the effectiveness of the start. (These points are not, one hopes, the most striking things you will have to say.)

There is no reason why a presentation cannot have two starts; something that was hinted at earlier. Begin, with some impact; quickly digress, so as to deal with administrative matters; then restart, with the restart becoming the real beginning. This is partly a matter of taste, but it is worth some thought, as a good start is useful in so many ways.

One administrative point no one minds hearing about concerns duration. It is slightly uncomfortable to sit and listen with no idea how long something is expected to last: 10 or 20 minutes, one or two hours? So you can usefully say, "I promise few things for the next hour, but one thing I do promise is to finish on time. You will be out of here by noon."

The meat of the matter: The middle

Here is the main part of your message, where the need for sound structure is greatest. This is the longest section of the presentation, in which you must:

- Put over the detail of your message
- Maintain attention and develop interest
- Do so in a way that continues to focus on the audience, reflecting their needs and situation

DEVISING A SOUND STRUCTURE

Some presenters have what might be called an "And another thing ..." style. They move from one thing to another and, although they identify separate points, they give no clue as to any overarching structure. What structure there may be is obscured by the push from "And now ..." to "And next ...".

The rules here are clear.

- You must originate a clear structure, and keep it firmly in mind throughout
- If necessary, you must explain the logic: "I am taking things in this order, so that ..."
- Early on, you must spell out to the audience what your chosen structure is to be (in whatever degree of detail is appropriate)
- You must guide the audience along by regular signposting
- You must link appropriately to any visual aids (or handouts); it can be confusing if you say, "Next, I want to move on to costing," but the slide reads, "Financial considerations"

All these allow the audience to keep things in context as the message builds up, as well as preventing you from rambling, and so being difficult to follow.

The job here is to move from point to point in a way that does each one justice, maintains continuity, and creates a good overall message. On the other hand, the intention is not to create a straitjacket. You need to maintain some flexibility, and you may wish to retain the ability to surprise the group, by not spelling out everything that is to come.

There are still a number of points to bear in mind if you are to get through the middle of your presentation smoothly. These points are dealt with now as dos and don'ts.

PRESENTING THE MIDDLE: WHAT TO DO

- **Always be clear.** Communication is inherently difficult, in the sense that there are plenty of possibilities for misunderstanding. Remember that it is *your* responsibility to make things clear. It is no good thinking, "What's the matter with these people? Are they all idiots?" when it is you who is being vague or obtuse. So, actively seek to be clear, and remember that it makes an excellent impression if people expect something to be complicated, and then find it easier than they thought. Make sure to worry about the little things as much as the big. If you have some highly complex points to make, you will be inclined to think hard about them, but you may drop in a phrase that, simply through lack of thought and so precision, dilutes understanding

- **Maintain the audience focus.** This point has been made already, but warrants repetition. It is vital to be seen to be directing what you do accurately, in light of the circumstances of the people in the audience

- **Be descriptive.** Presentations should paint a picture. This can be done in various ways: by simile ("It is like ...") – the better the comparison made, the more powerful the point; or by using a good turn of phrase, which may be emphasized by visual aids (see below)

- **Be memorable.** Not in every word you say, which would be an impossible task, but by building in some especially apt, or telling, phrases. You can also repeat such phrases, for example, by using them, maybe in different ways, as part of your signposting

- **Use visual aids.** These may be in the form of slides, or they may be more in the nature of exhibits (such as product samples). Whatever they may be, visual aids are important. They add variety, focus the message, and assist description – sometimes dramatically. We all know the way that a graph, for instance, can put over a point in a moment that would take much longer to explain in words alone. More of visual aids on pages 153–154.

- **Use your physical manner to enhance your message.** Enthusiasm is part of this process, as are gestures and general animation. Later in this Step, we discuss in more detail how you can use your physical manner to benefit a presentation

- **Offer proof where necessary.** If you seek agreement from people, remember that you cannot simply set out the facts as you see them. If you say, "It is a very practical solution," the response may well be, "You would say that, wouldn't you?" Adding other opinions, citing references, and using empirical results will all strengthen your argument. If you make presentations that must be persuasive, there are separate skills here that may be worth checking out

- **Use your voice.** This is obviously your greatest asset in presenting. Variety, pace, and emphasis are all essential, and these elements and more can continuously strengthen your presentational power
- **Use, and show, a "master plan."** If there is particular complexity or need for clarity, it may be worth having one overall visual aid (a slide or flip-chart sheet, perhaps) that acts as the "contents page" for your presentation. This can be reshown, being used to punctuate the proceedings, so as to recap, ensure things remain in context, look ahead, and lead on to the next point

PRESENTING THE MIDDLE: WHAT NOT TO DO

Conversely, there are numbers of things to watch out for and avoid. These include the following.

- **Unnecessary verbal padding.** Here, I am thinking not so much of rambling (though this is obviously to be avoided) but of words such as the ubiquitous "basically" (used at the start of every other sentence, this is both superfluous and annoying) and phrases like "due to the fact that ..." (when "because" will do nicely). You can doubtless think of more examples

- **Overuse of jargon.** This is sometimes described as "professional shorthand." Every field has its own version of jargon, and, in its place, jargon can be useful. For instance, why say four words if you can replace them with an abbreviation or acronym, consisting of four initials? But, and it is a big but, jargon only works when people all understand – otherwise it confuses and dilutes meaning. Moreover, jargon, if used inappropriately, can be regarded as disrespectful by certain groups of people. A surfeit of it, and your message is lost. This is a common error; if necessary, take advice from a recovering jargonaholic. The principle here (and regarding the points below) is similar to that for written communication

- **Vague or bland terminology.** What does it mean to say that something is "quite nice," "rather large," or "very good"? If the point is unimportant, then these descriptions might be sufficient, but if a more powerful point is being made, then these descriptions should be avoided

- **Unwarranted assumptions.** These include assumptions about anything to do with your audience that you do not know factually, such as their views, fears, or prejudices, or their level of knowledge or experience. Predicating what you say on something known to be false hardly increases your impact; more so when people believe you should have known the facts of the matter

Following these rules can ensure that the audience is happy, or at least content, to follow your progress. You are well on your way to achieving your aims. But there is one more thing that needs doing if you are to stay on track.

OBSERVING AND USING FEEDBACK

Even when you are not seeking participation, there are signs from any group to guide you and, if you are quick on your feet, to enable you to fine-tune what you still have to do.

Both listen and watch for any hints about how your audience is reacting. Ask yourself questions like these.

- Are they fidgeting or restless?
- Are they nodding or whispering together?
- Can I invite feedback, perhaps with a quick question and a show of hands?
- Can I anticipate any objections and snuff them out fast? ("I'll bet you're thinking this is just too complicated. Seems that way, but let me show you how ...")

Some observations obviously indicate positive feedback; others may need double-checking. A whispered comment to a neighbor may be, "That's a good point" or, "Did you watch TV last night?" Others may be obviously negative, but provide useful feedback – at worst, to duck incoming missiles! As Bob Hope once said of audiences in his early days, "If they liked you, they didn't applaud – they just let you live."

The reassurance provided by any positive feedback is clearly likely to boost confidence. If some adjustment is necessary, then the options element of your speaker's notes may prove a useful starting point for deciding what must be done "on the run."

A happy ending

There is satisfaction in a happy ending. Threads come together, conclusions are reached, and everything is generally wrapped up. The end of a presentation, like the beginning, is important – disproportionately so – and may need special thought to get it right.

The intentions are clear, namely to:

- Make any final points and summarize
- Meet the brief (drawing conclusions, making recommendations, or whatever is required)
- End on a positive – and, if possible, high – note

The overall intention is to finish up a presentation that is felt to have achieved its objectives for its audience.

So first decide what the end point is. Your objectives, and the logic and structure of what you have been going through, will usually lead on naturally to an end point. There is a significant opportunity here. Summarizing effectively is not the easiest thing to do. Because it is found difficult by many people, effective summarizing impresses when it is well done. The effort of creating this impression is worth making. It can be easy to spoil a good ending, so here are some don'ts.

- **Do not** seem to end and yet continue, saying "finally" three times before rambling on to some new digression
- **Do not** rush for the end (because time is running out,

or out of sheer relief), and let it become disjointed and confused

- **Do not** repeat points inappropriately in summary. The end means what it says, and is not an excuse to revisit half the presentation

- **Do not** make "Thank you" the last thing you say. This can lead to a tailing-away. Even if there is a powerful conclusion,it will run into the sand if you say, "Thank you very much for the opportunity. I am grateful for your time and ..." I am not advising that a thank you be omitted when it is called for, only that it not be placed last. A more suitable approach might be to say, "Well, I am grateful for your time. Thank you for listening – I will end with one final thought ..."

A SIGN-OFF PHRASE

At the end of the end, you need a neat way of signing off. A sign-off phrase may dwell in the minds of the audience longer than some of the other things you say, so it should be appropriate and, on occasion, memorable.

The techniques involved in winding up are very much like those suggested for use at the beginning of the beginning – asking the audience a question, quoting something, and so on – to which might be added the device of urging them to act.

TIMING

The key to successful comedy, it is said, is timing. It is important in presenting, too. And, at the end, the rule here is simple: *always finish on time.* Good timekeeping is a discipline for you, but it is a courtesy and, perhaps more importantly, it impresses. Start by saying, "And, in the half hour I have, I ... ," and add toward the end, "I see my time is almost up, so ... ," and you will gain additional respect. You also avoid the very real hazard of people starting to think about the time ("Five minutes over time already; I wonder how much longer ...") in a way that acts as a distraction.

Sometimes, however, things conspire to handicap your ability to keep to time.

The unforeseen

All sorts of things can happen along the way to create interruptions. Expect them, and they will not surprise and throw you. And another rule: *never compete with an interruption.* If someone comes into the room with coffee on a cart, and begins to make a noise, acknowledge and deal with it: "Perhaps we can break for a moment while arrangements for refreshments are made." People will simply think it odd if you assume it is not distracting and plow on regardless. I once missed the punch line of what gave every appearance of being a good joke when a presenter ignored an aircraft overhead and became, for a few moments, inaudible. I still resent it.

! A chairperson can be called upon to help deal with an interruption.
● Ask: "Do you want me to pause for a moment?" They may then stop the

**interruption or organize a momentary
break.**

Audience control is also important. If you are the sole presenter and there is no chair, you effectively have the role of chair, and can decide and say firmly how things like questions will be dealt with. For example, questions can be held until the right moment, or dealt with after the formal proceedings have finished (on time).

And that, as they say, is all there is to it – or not, as the case may be. I'm afraid there is more to come, quite a bit more, all of which has to be borne in mind, and all of which can influence the final outcome and make your presentations successful.

Let us end this section with an analogy. Can you drive a car? Do you remember learning to drive? (Imagine, if you do not drive, some similarly complex skill.) You doubtless recall a stage when you became convinced that driving was an impossibility.

If you were anything like me, you went through one stage convinced that the plethora of things that had to be done at once – steering, changing gear, watching the road, signaling (and thinking, for goodness' sake!) – was simply too much. Driving was clearly not possible, either physically or mentally! But, finally, it all came together. For the experienced driver, while driving always demands concentration, some aspects of it become second nature. Driving really is possible, and everything it entails really can all happen at once.

Presenting is in some ways similar. There is a good deal not only to think about, but also to do, and seemingly simultaneously. Let me assure the less experienced presenter that, with practice, the techniques involved here do come together, in the same way that those in driving do. A sound knowledge of what is involved is the first step to putting it all together.

I said there was more to come; there is. In the next section, we look at a variety of ways in which power and precision can be added to what a presenter does.

ADDING POWER AND PRECISION

A presentation must be well prepared and well structured, but it needs to be more than these if it is to have a real spark of life.

The presenters' maxim makes it all sound so simple: stand up, look them in the eye, and let them have it! Unfortunately, there are a significant number of details that, together and separately, can act to add to what might otherwise be a serviceable, but routine, presentation.

In view of the number, I had better start with some of my own medicine, and lay down some signposting. Based on the short maxim above, there are four main topics to consider. (I have divided "let them have it" in two.) These are:

- Feet and stance
- Eyes, and eye contact
- Hands and arms, and gestures with them
- Voice and sound

Let us take each in turn.

Feet and stance

The question of feet may seem like a minor detail, but your footwork influences your stance, and hence your style, and it can also keep you comfortable.

Consider first *where* you stand. There are a variety of options that you can choose from, or that you may have to cope with, if you are not responsible for organizing the presenting environment. Whether you are on a conference platform (perhaps behind a lectern or table) or inside a U-shaped layout (perhaps in front of a table), you will be confronted with slightly different problems and opportunities. There is more security behind a table with a lectern to hold on to, but there may be more rapport with a group if you are located among them. Certainly, each option needs differing organization. If you wish to be mobile, then you can carry a clipboard with you. If you are content to stay put, then you need have no more before you than a fistful of loose papers.

Once you have decided where to stand, you can think of exactly how you need to conduct yourself there.

The first rule is to *stand up straight*. You want to look smart and alert, not slovenly and slouching. Keeping your feet a little apart is the most comfortable position, especially if you have to stand for any length of time.

The second rule is to *move*. Standing rigidly does not just look uncomfortable; it is uncomfortable. Worse, a static pose can engender a static delivery. Some degree of movement will:

- Help facilitate a style that includes an appropriate number of gestures
- Help maintain attention on you
- Enable you to undertake comfortably any tasks that demand mobility (there is no point in straining to reach the projector to change a slide, if taking a step is all that is necessary to make it easy)

You can overdo movement, though. Too much, and you may appear nervous, distract people, find yourself in the wrong place at the wrong moment, or trip over yourself as you rush to change the next slide. A balance is best, but some movement is essential – for you and the audience.

Eyes, and eye contact

Think of some of the ways in which you do not want to be perceived – as anxious, nervous, incompetent, lacking credibility, rigid in your approach, or uninterested in the audience. You get the idea. The surest way to encourage such feelings is by avoiding eye contact.

Good eye contact takes a little effort, but will rapidly become habitual. It should be comprehensive, taking in the whole group (or all parts of a large audience), and it should be deliberate and seen as intentional; though it should not become so regular in pattern as to suggest to the audience a set routine rather than openness and care.

Openness and care are very valuable in this respect. They increase audience focus and rapport, seem to display confidence, allow greater assertiveness where appropriate, and, coupled with the right expression (whether that be a smile or a look of serious concentration), can make all the difference to the way a speaker is viewed.

Hands and arms, and gestures with them

"What do I do with my hands?" is a common cry of the inexperienced speaker. And, granted, if your hands *do look* awkward, then they may project a lack of confidence or authority, which is best avoided. Unfortunately, thinking about your hands too much tends to compound any awkwardness. The best advice may be to forget them.

However, that is easier said than done, so here are some suggestions if you can't forget them. Cultivate a suitable resting position, for instance, with one hand on the lectern and the other hand by your side. Bear in mind that having one hand in your pocket looks acceptable, but having both hands in your pockets looks slovenly. Folded arms look defensive and reduce rapport with your audience.

That said, the best approach is to give your hands something to do. For example:

- Hold something, such as a pen, a reminder card, or a clipboard
- Keep your hands and arms busy making gestures

But remember what they say: moderation in all things. And so it is with gestures of the hands and arms. Too many, and they distract; too few, and again they distract, as well as giving out a feeling of uncertainty.

Two levels of gesture are important. First, relax, be comfortable (without thinking about it too much), and allow the normal movements that accompany conversation to occur naturally.

Secondly, intentionally exaggerate selected movements to emphasize what you are saying, perhaps by:

- Pointing to a slide or a member of the group
- Indicating size as you mention, "Vast costs"
- Counting on your fingers as you utter, "First, ... Secondly, ..."

Or, more dramatically, by:

- Sweeping items, real or imaginary, off a table
- Banging your fist on the table to underline a negative point

What works best here *flows* – a comfortable resting position, some regular natural movement, occasional intended and specific gestures, and back to resting.

Voice and sound

Presentation does not require a special voice. Indeed, it would be difficult to sustain something artificial throughout a whole presentation. What is necessary, however, might best be described as an exaggeration of various elements of voice. You should try to do the following.

- **Speak up.** You need to be audible, but without straining to be so. In a normal room (where there is no need for a microphone), you should simply be conscious of addressing those furthest from you. If there were only two of you, at either end of the room, you would do this entirely without effort.

- **Place the emphasis accurately.** This applies to both:
  - words: "*place* the emphasis accurately"/"place the emphasis *accurately*"
  - phrases: some passages of what you present are more important than others, and how you say them should make this clear. You can couple verbal emphasis with signposting: "Now this is a key point ..."

In addition, the power of your voice affects emphasis. An extra-firm tone acts to increase importance, as does lowering the voice. Think of the movies – the most menacing villain is often soft-spoken.

- **Pause, regularly.** Any nervousness tends to make you omit pauses. Regular pausing may take conscious effort. Remember that what seems a long time to you may only be a moment. A pause is very useful for:
  - letting something sink in
  - focusing attention
  - adding drama (the classic dramatic pause)
  - providing break points to separate different issues
  - giving you time to think, monitor progress, or check timing
- **Remember punctuation.** Try not to draw breath where there is no clear pause, and make sure to pause for sufficient time where there should be a comma, colon, semicolon, or period

- **Choose your words carefully.** This links to both preparation and pace. If you are ill prepared and rushing along, the words can become serviceable ("This is important ..."), rather than precise and appropriate ("This can have a catastrophic effect ..."). Detail is important here. Just one word may make *some* difference or a *powerful* difference

- **Speak clearly.** To impress, you must be heard and understood. Do not mumble. Exaggerate your clarity of speech, especially for items like figures. Effort here may act to slow you down a little, which may be no bad thing

- **Remember pitch and inflection.** The pitch of your voice carries meaning, so a squeaky-sounding eruption may have none of the power you intended it to have. Inflection can be used to convey meaning as well. Are people clear that something is a question? That is, can they hear the question mark?

There may seem to be a great many things to get your head around here, but all of them can be improved with practice that cultivates the right habits. The overall effect must aim to be seamless and, in some respects, effortless. If your objectives are clear, if you have a structure to follow, and if you know which points you want to emphasize, then you will fall into a natural rhythm, which adds pace, variety and emphasis as you go.

Two final touches

There are two further ways of adding to the power, pace, and variety of what you do: with a little (more) drama or some humor.

 Use drama and humor carefully, but do not overdo them either.

Let us take each in turn.

A LITTLE DRAMA

This can involve a number of things – and be as simple as the dramatic pause – but often comprises exaggeration of voice and gesture, and sometimes both. Examples include the following.

- **A simple phrase delivered with emphasis and/or the use of repetition** (especially at the end of a sentence). "So this is something we should not put up with – *not for a single moment!*"
- **A really exaggerated gesture.** "This is enough to make anyone exhausted!" (The presenter sits/collapses in the chair for a moment, before standing slowly and continuing in a measured manner.)
- **Something unashamedly theatrical.** For example, I conduct courses on writing sales letters, and will sometimes tear something up ostentatiously, flinging it with great satisfaction into a wastebasket – to make the

point that such correspondence must earn a reading, and has consequences if it fails to do so

You may be able to think of other examples of dramatic flourishes, and you may want to try them in a way that fits your style of presentation. However, do not attempt anything too elaborate without care, practice, or both – if the flourish falls flat, it will dilute the overall effect you are having.

SOME HUMOR

There is, or should be, opportunity for light moments in many business presentations. "Now, did you hear about the farmer who had a pig with a wooden leg?" But, I digress. As you can probably tell, injecting humor can create dangers.

Saying, "Now, here's a funny story ... ," effectively alerting people to the fact that a good laugh is imminent, and then failing to fetch a laugh, certainly creates an anticlimax and perhaps an awkward moment. More so if what is said is not only unfunny, but also inappropriate or embarrassing.

Be careful of anything that, by its very nature, is difficult to pull off. For example, if something is in the nature of a tongue-twister, if it demands a particular accent, or if it typically prompts heckling, then it is probably best avoided.

Some things are safer. A quotation ("As Gore Vidal said of Eisenhower, the former president was 'reading a speech with his usual sense of discovery'") may raise a smile, if not a laugh, and make a point. And if it only makes a point, no great harm is done. A less-than-serious phrase (likening a difficulty to "nailing jam to the wall"), while it may not raise a laugh or even a smile (or be intended to), may still give some useful light relief. This is yet another thing that comes back to preparation, and which is also possible if you are feeling quick on your feet at a suitable moment.

Jokes have their place, of course. It would be a dull old world if no business presentation had appropriate room for an unashamed digression. But, in my experience, jokes work best if they do make a point, even if a somewhat contrived or distant one. And they should be tested. Try them out on a few people – not just one polite person – to reduce any risk of failure.

Keeping a note of them, too, may be useful (something I have always meant to do more surely). Like fashion, their day will come again, and a story that makes a good point while discussing financial matters, say, may be used again in due course; though not, perhaps, with the same audience.

Appropriately used humor is certainly useful. As well as creating an immediate impact, it serves as dramatic punctuation. After the digression, you start again, and pick up the next main point, with suitable emphasis.

A VISUAL ELEMENT
Perhaps the most important visual aid has already been mentioned, namely, you. Numbers of factors, such as hand/arm gestures and dramatic flourishes, are part of this, as are your general manner and appearance.

More tangible forms of visual aid are also important. Such things as slides serve several roles, which include:

- Focusing attention within a group
- Helping to change pace and add variety
- Giving a palpably visual aspect to something
- Acting as signposts to where, within its structure, a presentation is at

They also help the presenter, providing reminders – over and above speaker's notes – of what comes next.

Be careful. Visual aids should *support* a message, not lead or overwhelm it. Just because slides exist, or are easy to originate, does not mean they will be right. You need to start by looking at the message, at what you are trying to do, and see what will help put it over and have an additive effect. Visual aids can make a point that is otherwise difficult or impossible to describe, in the way that a graph might make an instant point that would otherwise be lost in a mass of figures. Or you may have a particular reason to use visual aids, perhaps to help get a large amount of information over more quickly.

Whatever visual aid you are using, remember to talk to the group, not to the visual aid. Looking at the screen too much when an overhead projector is being used is a common fault. Make sure that visuals are visible (do not get in the way of them yourself); explain them or their purpose, as necessary; mention whether or not you will be handing out paper copies of them; and stop visuals distracting by removing them as soon as you are finished with them.

General principles of using visual aids

- Keep the content simple
- Restrict the amount of information and the number of words
  - to give structure, use headings, single words, or short statements
  - avoid the appearance of clutter and complexity
  - use a running logo, for example, the main heading/topic on each slide
- Use diagrams and graphs where possible, rather than too many figures; and never read figures out loud without visual support
- Build in variety within the overall theme, for example, with color or variations of the form of aid used
- Emphasize the theme and structure, for example, by regularly using a single aid to recap the agenda or objectives
- Ensure that the content of the visuals matches the words
- Make sure that the content is necessary and relevant
- Check that everything is visible. Ask yourself, "Is it clear? Will it work in the room? Does it suit the equipment?" (Colors and the right-sized typeface help here.)
- Ensure that the layout emphasizes the meaning you want, and not some minor detail
- Select the right aid for the right purpose

Using an overhead projector

Some care should be taken in using an overhead projector

to begin with; it appears deceptively simple, but presents hazards to the unwary. The following tips may well be useful.

- Make sure that the electrical cord is out of the way, or taped to the floor. Falling over it will improve neither your presentation nor your dignity

- Check that the overhead projector works before you start using it with the group. This also goes for the second bulb (and a spare, even) and for the roll of acetate film (if you are using one to write *ad hoc* notes; this is particularly useful in answering questions)

- Ensure that the overhead projector is positioned where you want; that it is within reach; and that it gives you room to move, as well as space alongside for papers. (Note: it may need to be in a slightly different place for left- and right-handed people – a hazard for some team presentations.)

- Stand back, and to the side of the overhead projector. Be sure not to obscure the view of the screen for anyone in the group

- Make sure that the picture is in focus. Then look primarily at the machine, rather than at the screen. The primary advantage of the overhead projector is to keep you facing the front

- Only use slides that have big enough typefaces or images, and, if you plan to write on acetate, check how large your handwriting needs to be

- Switch off the overhead projector when changing slides, so as to avoid the jumbled image that appears as slides are changed while it is switched on

- To project the image on a slide progressively, cover the bottom part of the image on the machine with a sheet of paper. Use paper that is not too thick, and you can still see the whole image through it, even though the whole image is not projected. As you slide the paper down, put a weight on it, to stop it from reaching the point where it must be held if it is not to fall off
- For handwritten use, fit an acetate roll to the overhead projector. This minimizes the amount of acetate used (which would otherwise be expensive), and removes to need to keep changing loose sheets
- Remember that when something new is shown, all attention is, at least momentarily, on it – so pause as a new image is shown, or what you say may be missed
- Add emphasis by highlighting certain things on the slides as you go through them. If you slip the slide under the acetate roll, you can do this without adjustment and without marking the slide
- Add information by showing two slides together (or by using an overlay attached to a slide and folded across). Alternatively, one slide may have minimal information on it – with such things as a title talk, session heading, or company logo remaining in view on it – as other slides are shown by being placed over it
- To point something out, lay a small pointer or pencil on the overhead projector. Extending pointers are, in my view, almost impossible to use without appearing pretentious, and they risk you turning your back on the group unnecessarily

Using PowerPoint

PowerPoint is a computer program that allows you to prepare slides on your computer, and project them through a projector, using the computer to control the show. So far so good. The program works well, and you have the ability to use a variety of layouts, colors, illustrations, and so on at the touch of a button.

There are some dangers, however (and many of the points made in reviewing the use of an overhead projector apply equally here). The first danger is not to get carried away by the technology. Not everything it can do is useful – certainly not all on one slide or even in one presentation – and it is a common error to allow the ease of preparation to increase the amount you have on a slide to the point where it becomes cluttered and difficult to follow. PowerPoint's technology might also lead you to use too many slides. Similarly, if you are going to use the program's various features, like the ability to strip in one line and then another to make up a full picture, remember to keep it manageable. Details here can be important, for instance, the choice of colors is prodigious, but not all the colors are equally suitable for making things clear.

The second danger is simply the increased risk of technological complexity. Sometimes, it is a simple error. Recently, I saw an important presentation have to proceed without the planned slides because the projector (resident at the venue) could not be connected to the laptop computer (which had been brought to the venue), because the electrical cords were incompatible. At other times, problems may be caused by something buried in the software. Again, not long ago I sat through a presentation that used 20 or 30 slides. Each time the slide was changed, there was an unplanned delay of three or four seconds. It was felt unwarranted to stop and risk tinkering with the equipment, but long before the 45-minute presentation finished, everyone in the group had lost patience.

So make sure (check, check, check ...) before a presentation that everything works. Run off transparencies that can be shown on an overhead projector, or paper handouts, as a sensible insurance in the event of disaster striking. Finally, follow all the overall rules, and do not forget that you do not have to have a slide on all the time – when you have finished with one, blank out the screen until you are ready for the next, so that the slide does not distract. Just pressing the "B" key on your computer does this, while pressing it again returns you to the next slide.

Automatic pilot

At this point, it is worth emphasizing one factor about the way visual aids are originated, one that can influence a presentation and dilute its effectiveness.

There are no doubt reasons, not least lack of time, but some presentations suffer not from poor decisions as their originators prepare them, but from no decision. They are assembled on automatic pilot, as it were, without thought and with certain habits perpetuated, regardless of how their deployment may suit the audience and affect the outcome. Various habits may be involved here; one is overwhelmingly in evidence. What is it? Well, it is positively motivated. Everyone knows that presentations are improved when they incorporate visual aids. The principle is sound, but still it matters how the visual aids are originated and deployed.

What tends to happen? Too often, the magic word is "PowerPoint."

Imagine: "he who must be listened to' stands at the front of the room, surrounded by equipment and with the screen glowing behind him. The audience is spellbound. The little company logo at the corner of the screen fascinates them. Every time the presenter clicks the computer mouse, and sends another yellow bullet point shuttling onto the screen from stage left, their attention soars. Here is what they see:

Main heading
- This is a bullet point
- This is another
- This is another
- This is one more
- And this is yet another
- And this is a bullet point as well
- And this ...

But you get the idea. In turn, one slide replaces another, then another replaces that, and another ... enough said. All are bland, all are simple checklists, yet the presenter finds them riveting; certainly, he spends most of his time looking over his shoulder at the screen, rather than at the audience. There is so much text on some slides that they are like pages out of a book, and an unsuitably small typeface compounds the effect, overburdening the minds of the audience. So he reads them, verbatim, more slowly than the audience does and with a tonethat leads one to suspect that he is seeing them for the first time. It becomes akin to a bureaucratic rain dance: a mantra and format are slavishly, indeed, unthinkingly, followed – yet at the end, no one is truly satisfied. The opportunity for a successful presentation – the open goal – is missed.

If only good business presentations were that easy, so mechanistic: put up one slide, read it out loud – repeat, and success follows automatically. But they are not. Large numbers of lackluster, wordy slides do not a good presentation make. Certainly, they do not make a distinctive or memorable one. But then, perhaps, in all honesty, "he who must be listened to" did not really believe they would do so. The slides are there because *that is how presentations are prepared*. An ubiquitous norm is followed largely unthinkingly, and the results fail to sparkle. Indeed, they may fail to explain, inform, or persuade.

Remember, the most important thing about visual aids is that they support what you want to say; they, and how they are produced, should not take over, so that they dictate how the presentation must be made.

It is quite useful to have a simple pie chart in mind as you prepare: one with just two divisions, indicating how much of the effect you aim for will come from the visuals, and how much from you.

Now, a further note of caution.

Beware gremlins

Is it Murphy's Law? Undoubtedly, it is an accurate maxim that if something can go wrong, it will; and nowhere is this more true than with equipment.

The moral: check, check, and check again. Everything – from the spare overhead-projector bulb (do not even think about using an old machine with only one bulb) to which way up 35mm slides are going to be, even whether the pens for the flip chart still work – is worth checking. A key element in the days of PowerPoint is the profusion of electrical cords connecting various machines. If you are taking a laptop to a meeting room in a hotel, and know that they have a projector you can use, make sure that you can connect to it.

Always double-check anything with which you are unfamiliar, especially if, with something like a microphone, what you do is going to be significantly dependent on it. And remember that while the sophistication of equipment increases all the time – with things like a laptop computer linked to a projector allowing first-class colored graphics to be projected at the touch of a button – so do the number of things that can potentially go wrong.

The concept of contingency is worth a thought: what do you do if disaster does strike? You have been warned.

Anything and everything

Finally, be inventive. Practically anything can act as a visual aid, from another person (carefully briefed to play their part) to an exhibit of some sort. In a business presentation, exhibits may be obvious items: products, samples, posters, and more – or maybe something totally unexpected.

There are hotels and conference centers whose proud boast is that access and strength allow you to say, "What we need now is some really heavyweight support," as a baby elephant walks across the platform behind you.

Like all the skills of presentations, while the basics give you a sound foundation, they can benefit from a little imagination.

KEY ISSUES

A word of summary: the following does not attempt to be comprehensive, revisiting everything, but rather to touch on certain key issues with an eye on increasing the likelihood of your presentations getting better and better.

Consider the alternatives: Dangers or opportunities

The dangers of poor presentations do not need reiterating in detail; it is enough to say that they have both business elements (not meeting your objectives or achieving what you want in terms of results and actions) and personal elements (which range from feeling mildly inadequate to seeing a rapid death as preferable to continuing to speak for another moment).

Both are to be avoided.

The incentives to avoid the dangers are very real. Presentational skills provide opportunities, and can sometimes do so in a major way – by means of the "open goal" referred to earlier. Once acquired, these skills can help you in your job, in your career, and in achieving things large and small, in both the long and short term.

So presentational skills are worth working at; although you may not achieve the standard you want in an instant or without some effort, remember the wise words of Ann Landers: "Opportunities are usually disguised as hard work, so most people don't recognize them." In fact, you may quickly turn in a workmanlike standard, and be surprised at just what you can achieve.

Deal with the negatives

Accept that – for whatever reason – most people seem to anticipate at least some difficulty with presentations (certainly early on). Accept also that there are many disparate matters that can conspire to make it more difficult to present effectively. But work to defuse such factors. The balance analogy made earlier in this Step can be of help. So can the idea of mental reach: your mind can only stretch itself around so many things at once. It is a bit like a juggler, with a number of balls in the air at the same time, who may find that faults – even tiny ones – quickly add up, and that they drop not just one ball, but several, or all, of the balls.

Similarly, if a part of your mind is busy thinking,

"What do I do with my hands?" then there is a little less of it available to focus on delivering an appropriate message in the right way. So every problem, or potential problem, that you deal with, in whatever way ("I'm comfortable with one hand on the lectern and the other holding a pen"), reduces the feeling of pressure of trying to concentrate on a dozen things at once and *yet still* deliver the presentation.

The first step to success here is simply to adopt a way of approaching any problems or negatives. This leads to dealing with the negatives one by one, until they are of insufficient weight to undermine in any serious way what you are trying to do. Of course, you cannot reduce all of them completely. Certainly, few people ever get over some feeling of nervousness, particularly as they start to speak; indeed, many people would say that a little apprehension at that stage is a good thing – the adrenaline it produces is necessary to the job to be done.

! If feeling nervous still worries you, at least label it positively. I once heard one speaker claim that he never had nerves, but that he admitted to a feeling of what he called "creative apprehension."

Study the skills

Earlier in this Step, it was said that presenting deserved both study and practice; by now (assuming you are still reading), you have at least done some study. There may be more to do, but certainly you will have been exposed to many of the fundamental principles that make for good presenting. Knowledge of these factors gives you something to aim for. If you understand the power of a dramatic pause, say, and how to hold it long enough to create the effect you want ... then there is more chance of you not only trying it, but also deploying it successfully. So, too, with the other tricks of the trade.

Never neglect preparation

George Bernard Shaw may have said, "The golden rule is that there are no golden rules," but here – to use an old device – there are three: preparation, preparation, and preparation.

It really does make all the difference.

To begin with, preparation may seem like a chore. Certainly, it can be time-consuming. But, if you evolve a systematic and consistent approach to how you prepare (in everything that I have said about preparation, I have been at pains to point out that your approach, while it must accommodate certain essentials, should above all suit *you*), then it will not only be useful, but will also get easier and quicker to do. Good preparation is a sound foundation for your presentations, and knowing that it has been thoroughly done is also a boost to your confidence.

Practice the skills

I have not disguised the fact that presentation is a practical business. Success cannot come solely from reading a book (though my intention was certainly that this should help); it also demands practice. Sometimes, this is in the form of rehearsal – trying it out in front of the mirror. It also involves learning from experience.

For some people, a good idea here is to *contrive* to increase the amount of practice they get. Let me explain what I mean. I know people who make few presentations; their jobs do not demand that they make more. Yet when they do give presentations, these are very important. So, in some organizations, steps are taken to get around the low rate of experience that results from this situation. For example, I have suggested to more than one of my clients that they use internal meetings to develop presentational skills. I can think of one client whose organization made it mandatory, at least for a while, for staff making formal inputs to internal meetings to stand up (and, in another case, to use at least one slide). The good results were noticeable; such actions accelerated the amount of practice enjoyed by staff, intensifying it over a short period of time, and improving their skills more quickly than would otherwise have been the case.

A similar argument might be advanced for certain more formal occasions or invitations. Are you, for instance, currently turning down requests to speak at events on the grounds that such jobs are not sufficiently important for you to take on, when it would be more accurate to say that you do not want, or do not have the confidence, to do them? What could or should you take on, in part for the experience it will give you? "No presentation, no practice"is hardly a recipe for improving standards.

There is another element of practice that should be

mentioned before we end, namely, training. The best training in making presentations involves skill development, and thus practice, and is done using video-recording equipment, so as to allow individual participants to see what they are doing and learn from having their practice critiqued. Each critique should be as much by the participant as by others. I conduct regular training courses in making presentations, both in the form of public seminars and in-company workshops. (There are, of course, many other providers of such training.) A training course can provide a short, sharp kick-start that, for some people, is invaluable. Sometimes, it can replace months of floundering around, uncertain quite how to improve what is being done. The payoff can be rapid and worth while, as, for example, with a customer presentation of some sort that successfully wins business. Training can be useful, whether you are making a start on the process or have some experience, but simply want to check and extend that experience. In common with other consultants, I regularly get asked to help with the preparation and rehearsal of particular presentations, for which short tutorial sessions, involving either groups or individuals, can be helpful and cost-effective.

Working on a presentation is certainly an activity in which you can get so close to things that you cannot see the forest for the trees, so an objective view (which might equally be from a colleague as from a consultant) can help move things along in a way that repeated private rehearsal may not.

FINALLY ...

A final few words: if you understand the principles involved (the tricks of the trade, as it were), and if you are well prepared in every sense (whether in having thought through what to say, how to say it, and what materials to have in front of you while you do so, or in having decided that you are comfortable with the environment and are not worried about how to stand, or whether your slides will be legible from the back of the room), then your presentation will stand a good chance of success.

Hopefully, this book has provided sufficient ideas and encouragement to get you started; indeed, to get you well under way. Even the most practiced and accomplished presenter can continue to learn for as long as they continue to present. So perhaps the last thing to be said is that you should actively plan to go on learning from experience. Good habits help here. If, after every presentation, there is something to note, and you make a point of noting it ("I must find a better way of explaining that" or "That's clearly a good description – I mustn't forget it"), then you will always be able to say that you were satisfied with your last presentation (even if never one hundred percent so). And that your next presentation will be even better.

So what next? Take a couple of deep breaths, maybe a sip of water, look your audience in their collective eyes, and begin: "Good morning ...".

> ! "Talking and eloquence are not the same: to speak, and to speak well, are two things."
>
> *Ben Jonson*

Afterword

❝Success doesn't come to you ... you go to it.**❞**

Marva Collins

Whatever form of communication you engage in, remember to think *before* you communicate. Preparation is the foundation for effective communication. It needs to be done, and requires time to be set aside in order to do it. Yet, on presentation-skills courses and elsewhere, I frequently hear people telling tales of woe about their experiences of giving presentations, and the same people then turn around and say, "There wasn't time to prepare properly." Allowing a presentation to go badly because of lack of preparation is sheer folly. Even a moment's thought, more so a reading of this book, will suggest that to embark on a presentation, or a piece of writing, well prepared is likely to enhance the chances of success.

What else makes the difference? Those who communicate best, and those whose profile is enhanced by what they do and how they do it, share the following attributes.

- They take on board the way in which things, such as a presentation or a report, are best done, allowing their knowledge to fuel their working

- They rate what they do as important, so they allow time for preparation, do things consciously, and anticipate how something will be received
- They act to accelerate their experience, considering self-critically how things have gone, analyzing what was good or less good, and adjusting what they do next in light of this process
- They let their approach feed their self-confidence, knowing that a presentation will go well if it has been well prepared, so creating a virtuous circle

An open goal presents an almost certain chance of scoring. So the right approach to communication will give you the best chances of success: being understood, obtaining agreement, impressing in whatever way you wish. That the right approach has been taken will be apparent to those who hear or read your messages. The messages will be cast in an accessible form, which has structure and logic, and uses real description rather than bland platitudes. They will, not least, command attention and, once the detail is taken in, be given due consideration.

The message and the messenger are inextricably linked. Confidence is read as authority, and this enhances attention and the chances of getting your message across. So does an appropriate degree of style. I remember attending a conference, where a row of speakers on the platform took turns to speak, introduced by a chair in the center of the platform. After the third speaker was introduced, he began, "I would like to address the subject of ——, and in the hour

I have to do so ..." The chair, sitting alongside, tugged at his sleeve, and the speaker paused, bent down, and listened to him for a moment. Standing up again, he continued, "I'm so sorry, in the 30 minutes I have available ... ," and, as he said this, he tore in two the sheets of paper he was holding, and tossed half of them over his shoulder. He got a murmur of laughter. More importantly, as I looked around the room, every single face seemed to be saying, "This looks like being good." He had the audience's total attention. Yet the gesture (no doubt contrived, but no less effective for that) had nothing to do with his topic; it simply positioned him as someone confident, who knew what he was doing.

Everyone can get something of this effect, just by thinking about how they will act, in order to produce something that will be well received. In this respect, everything contributes; in the words of a major supermarket, "Every little helps."

66 The ability to express an idea is almost as important as the idea itself. 99

Bernard Baruch

About the Author

Patrick Forsyth has himself had a successful career; or certainly he likes to think so. He now runs his own company, Touchstone Training & Consultancy, specializing in the improvement of marketing, sales, and communications skills, and says he has now "found an employer I can really get on with."

He began his career in publishing and worked happily in sales, in promotion and marketing there, before escaping to something better paid just ahead of terminal poverty. He then worked for the Institute of Marketing (now the Chartered Institute), first in research, latterly in the promotion of their training products and publications. He helped set up an export assistance scheme and then moved into consultancy, first in a management marketing position. Much against his better judgment initially, he was soon persuaded to get involved in client work and began to undertake consulting assignments and conduct training courses.

His work also began to take on an international

dimension. He helped set up offices in Brussels and Singapore and began to work and lecture overseas. He still travels regularly, especially to South East Asia, and has, over the years, worked in most countries in continental Europe, including the former Eastern Bloc. Other, more occasional, destinations have included America, Australia, East Africa, Argentina, and Borneo.

After some years at director level in a medium-sized marketing consultancy, he set up his own organization in 1990. He conducts training for organizations in a wide range of industries, and has conducted public courses for such bodies as the Institute of Management, the City University Business School, and the London Chamber of Commerce and Industry.

In addition, he writes on matters of management and marketing in a variety of business journals, and is the author of more than 50 business books, corporate publications and training material.

Books in the Business Solutions Series

EFFECTIVE DECISION MAKING
10 steps to better decision making and problem solving | Jeremy
Kourdi

BRILLIANT COMMUNICATION
5 steps to communicating your message clearly and effectively |
Patrick Forsyth

THE NEW RULES OF ENTREPRENEURSHIP
*What it really takes to become a savvy and successful
entrepreneur* | Rob Yeung

GREAT SELLING SKILLS
How to sell anything to anyone | Bob Etherington

THE NEW RULES OF JOBHUNTING
A modern guide to finding the job you want | Rob Yeung

MANAGE YOUR BOSS
How to create the ideal working relationship | Patrick Forsyth

GREAT NEGOTIATING SKILLS
The essential guide to getting what you want | Bob Etherington

SURVIVING OFFICE POLITICS
Coping and succeeding in the workplace jungle | Patrick Forsyth

ESSENTIAL TIME MANAGEMENT
How to become more productive and effective | Brett Hilder

SIMPLY A GREAT MANAGER
The fundamentals of being a successful manager | Mike Hoyle &
Peter Newman